The Smartest Kids

Don't Go to School

The Smartest Kids

Don't Go to School

Kytka Hilmar-Jezek

DISTINCT PRESS

Distinct Press Publishing.
www.distinctpress.com
US+ 727-238-7884

The views expressed in this work are the author's own and may not reflect the opinions or policies of any organization or individual. The author's personal experiences and opinions are shared for entertainment and educational purposes. Readers are encouraged to form their own conclusions based on the content presented. The author assumes no responsibility for the reader's actions. References to people, organizations, or events are based on the author's translation, recollection and/or interpretation. This work does not provide professional advice and readers should consult experts in relevant fields for guidance.

Library of Congress Cataloging-in-Publication Data

Hilmar-Jezek, Kytka 1964-
          The Smartest Kids Don't Go to School / Kytka Hilmar-Jezek

Summary: Awaken your child's genius and find answers to all your questions about unschooling in "The Smartest Kids Don't Go to School." This illuminating guide dives deep into the philosophy and practice of unschooling, offering practical insights on nurturing self-directed learning, fostering parent-teacher collaboration, and igniting curiosity. Explore the challenges of traditional schooling, navigate legalities, and uncover valuable resources for embarking on a transformative educational journey. Unlock your child's full potential and embrace a new paradigm of education with this comprehensive and enlightening book.

ISBN-13: 978-1-943103-12-6

1. EDUCATION / Homeschooling 2. FAMILY & RELATIONSHIPS / Parenting / Alternative Education 3. EDUCATION / Educational Policy & Reform / Alternative Education 4.

"The need for imagination, a sense of truth, and a feeling of responsibility—these three forces are the very nerve of education."

- Rudolf Steiner

Contents

Acknowledgments

I offer my heartfelt gratitude to Rudolf Steiner, whose profound philosophy has served as a guiding light throughout my journey. It is through his wisdom that I have come to grasp the true essence of education and the pivotal role of a teacher. Steiner's teachings have enlightened me to the fundamental truth that a teacher, who can assume any form, holds the sacred responsibility of nurturing within the child a lifelong passion for learning. His invaluable insights have shaped my understanding, inspiring me to embark on the path of education with unwavering dedication and a deep-rooted commitment to fostering the innate curiosity and love for knowledge that resides within each young mind.

Above all, my deepest gratitude goes to my three beloved children, who have now blossomed into remarkable individuals at the ages of 30, 25, and 22. When I embarked on this profound journey, the availability of information was scarce, but what prevailed was an unwavering trust in my instincts and a profound commitment to allowing you to flourish at your own pace and pursue your own passions.

In those formative days, a flicker of doubt would occasionally creep into my thoughts, causing me to question if I was, in fact, toying with the very fabric of your lives. However, as I witness the extraordinary intelligence, boundless compassion, resounding success, and unwavering love that radiates from each one of you, I am overwhelmed with joy and gratitude that we embarked on this shared path of growth and discovery. Being both your mother and teacher has been an unparalleled privilege, and I wholeheartedly thank each and every one of you for unveiling the depths of my being and igniting the very best within me.

Zachary, Zanna, Zynnia; My love for you all transcends the limitations of words...

Preface

During "Education is not the filling of a pail, but the lighting of a fire."
- William Butler Yeats

I have always found myself drawn to the exploration of alternative educational philosophies and practices, even before I had children of my own. Unschooling, with its simple yet profound premise, captured my attention. It is an idea that challenges the traditional notions of schooling and offers a refreshing perspective on education.

In the words of Margaret Mead, whose grandmother recognized the value of a true education and kept her out of school, "Unschooling is a simple and beautiful idea." However, for many, it requires a bit of explanation and understanding. That is precisely what this book aims to provide.

If you are reading this preface, chances are you are among the "Schooled" - individuals who have experienced the institutionalized system called "School" in your own lives. Research indicates that, for many children, the schooling experience is more disheartening than fulfilling, leaving them feeling humiliated and frustrated. Now, you have encountered the concept of "Unschooling" and find yourself wondering what life might have been like without the constraints of traditional schooling.

This book is written with you in mind, particularly if you are a parent or caregiver seeking the best educational path for your children. Its purpose is to introduce you to a body of thinking and real-life experiences that present a range of alternatives to the school system we were subjected to as children. Unschooling, by its very nature, rejects the limitations of standardized curricula, methodologies, and pedagogies. It challenges the validity of these concepts.

Throughout history and even today, being "Schooled" is often viewed positively, as something desirable or even essential, while being "Unschooled" has traditionally been perceived as a severe defect or handicap. This book aims to dismantle and deconstruct the prevailing dichotomy between Schooled and Unschooled, demonstrating that schooling and education are fundamentally at odds with each other. If, like Margaret Mead's wise grandmother, you truly desire education for your child or grandchild, then it is clear that the path of traditional schooling is not the way to achieve it.

Before we delve into the heart of the book, it is essential to address geography. The Unschooling movement originated in the United States, spearheaded by pioneers such as John Holt in the 1970s and continued by advocates like John Taylor Gatto around the turn of the millennium. Consequently, much of the literature and experiences shared in this book are centered around the American context. However, it is crucial to recognize that while the aspiration for universal schooling may vary from country to country, the principles and ideas discussed here hold relevance for readers worldwide, regardless of their location, whether in Afghanistan, Zimbabwe, or anywhere in between.

Regarding the structure of this book, it emerged organically from the incessant stream of questions I have been asked repeatedly. The initial edition of the book took the form of a long series of questions and answers, aiming to address the most common inquiries. However, in its current manifestation, I have meticulously crafted each idea and fragment of information into concise sections that possess the ability to stand independently.

This deliberate design has given rise to a comprehensive and expansive table of contents, enabling readers to swiftly locate the specific answers they seek. One notable advantage of this format is the freedom it affords, granting readers the autonomy to navigate through the book according to their own convenience. There is no compulsion to read it cover to cover, akin to immersing oneself in the narrative of a novel. While the book comprises distinct chapters, I have intentionally omitted a prescribed narrative sequence, fostering a sense of exploration and intellectual freedom.

I hope that this book will serve as a guide and catalyst for your exploration of unschooling and the possibilities it holds for transforming education. It is my intention to provide you with a comprehensive resource that addresses the common questions, concerns, and misconceptions surrounding unschooling.

Unschooling is not a one-size-fits-all approach. It embraces the uniqueness of each individual and recognizes that true education goes beyond the confines of a classroom. It encourages curiosity, self-directed learning, and the pursuit of passions and interests. Unschooling invites children to actively participate in shaping their educational journeys, fostering a love for learning that extends far beyond the boundaries of traditional schooling.

Throughout this book, you will find insights, anecdotes, and practical tips from experienced unschoolers, educators, and researchers. We will delve into the philosophical underpinnings of unschooling, explore its impact on socialization and academic progress, and provide guidance on navigating the practical aspects of an unschooling lifestyle. You will also discover inspiring stories of individuals who have embraced unschooling and thrived in their educational pursuits.

While unschooling challenges conventional norms, it is not without its own challenges and considerations. We will address common concerns such as college admissions, standardized testing, and the role of parents in the unschooling journey. By the end of this book, you will have gained a deeper understanding of unschooling and its potential to revolutionize the way we approach education.

It is my sincere hope that this book will empower you to question the prevailing notions of schooling and open your mind to the possibilities of unschooling. Whether you are a parent, educator, or simply curious about alternative educational approaches, I invite you to embark on this journey with an open heart and a willingness to embrace change.

Remember, education is not confined to the walls of a classroom or the pages of a textbook. It is a lifelong endeavor, driven by curiosity, passion, and a thirst for knowledge. Unschooling offers a pathway to true educational freedom, where learning becomes a joyful and meaningful experience.

Chapter 1 – Understanding Unschooling

Unschooling vs. Schooling

When I delve into the realm of unschooling, its stark contrast to traditional schooling becomes glaringly apparent. But "School" is a vast concept, encompassing a multitude of educational approaches that defy a singular, all-encompassing definition. From Montessori to Pestalozzi, Waldorf to Summerhill, the educational landscape teems with diverse forms of schooling. So, what does "School" truly mean?

In my quest for understanding, I turn to the words of Ivan Illich (1926-2002), a trailblazer in the deschooling movement of the 1970s, whose illuminating definition resonates deeply. Illich describes 'School' as "the age-specific, teacher-related process requiring full-time attendance at an obligatory curriculum."

Contemplating this definition, it becomes evident that the prevailing notion of School, widely accepted in our societies, dismisses any form of learning that is independent, voluntary, or devoid of the authoritarian presence of a trained and licensed figure—a 'teacher.' It also entails adherence to a predetermined set of instructions known as a 'curriculum,' which is not crafted by the teacher or developed collaboratively with the learners but rather dictated by central authorities.

This working definition effectively disregards any learning experiences that are not forced upon individuals through legal compulsion. Think of universities where attendance is a matter of personal choice or local 'schools of music' where children engage in musical pursuits purely for the love of it, rather than seeking a state-authorized certificate of musical competence.

With this understanding, the inherent constraints of traditional schooling come into focus—compulsory attendance, standardized curricula, and the authoritative presence of instructors. In contrast, unschooling operates beyond these limitations. It embraces self-directed learning, freedom of choice, and environments that transcend the confines of a conventional classroom.

As we embark on an exploration of unschooling within the pages of this book, I extend an invitation to you, dear reader, to join me in delving into its philosophical underpinnings, practical applications, and the profound potential it holds for transforming the educational landscape. By questioning the prevailing norms of schooling, we unlock a world of possibilities offered by unschooling—an approach that empowers learners and nurtures their individuality.

But what exactly does unschooling encompass? What is the unity and coherence that underlies its broad definition? It's only natural to ponder these questions. Unschooling encompasses educational and instructional activities that break away from the coercive nature of traditional schooling. Yet, one might question whether this expansive definition leads to a lack of unity or a clear framework. Can any activity involving a child be considered part of unschooling as long as it avoids coercion, age-group restrictions, full-day immersion, and the presence of a teacher, as outlined by Ivan Illich?

Indeed, that is the very essence of unschooling.

While the concept may initially appear boundless, a discernible thread of unity and coherence emerges. Unschooling, at its core, vehemently rejects coercion, standardization, and the rigid grip of centralized systems. It stems from a profound understanding that education is, at its heart, a deeply personal journey—a journey undertaken by individuals who resist being confined to predetermined molds.

Furthermore, individuals are not faceless entities lost in the vast expanse of bureaucracy; they exist within the tapestry of their local contexts. It is within this realm of freedom and openness that unschooling thrives. It refuses to impose a single approach or suppress individuality; instead, it revels in the splendid tapestry of human diversity.

Unschooling is as diverse as the individuals it embraces, intentionally so. For instance, a child is encouraged to embrace the joy of reading when they are genuinely ready and captivated, not when an arbitrary timetable dictates. They are free to pursue a myriad of interests that align with their inclinations—a dance of free play, the art of invention, the wonders of scientific experimentation, the realms of video games, the lessons of friendship, the depths of spiritual exploration, the pursuit of athletics, and the cultivation of trust in oneself and others.

The true beauty of unschooling lies in its adaptability to the unique passions and developmental paths of each individual. It nurtures exploration, self-discovery, and a holistic approach to learning that encompasses an array of diverse activities. By casting aside coercion, children are empowered to engage in pursuits that resonate with their authentic passions, fostering a lifelong love affair with learning.

While the concept of unschooling may, at first glance, appear multifaceted, it rests upon the principles of individuality, freedom, and non-coercion. By embracing the unity that resides within the splendid diversity of unschooling, we can redefine education as a personalized odyssey guided by a child's passions and fueled by their intrinsic motivation.

Unschooling challenges the established paradigms of education and presents an alternative that honors and nurtures the unique strengths and interests of each individual. By recognizing the harmony concealed within the kaleidoscope of unschooling, we unlock its transformative potential and grant individuals the power to shape their educational journeys with intention and purpose.

Together, let us embark on this journey of exploration, seeking to unravel the intricacies and nuances of unschooling. As we venture forth, we will strive to discover the unity and coherence that lie within this transformative approach to education.

The Many Faces of Unschooling

Unschooling, as a concept, has traversed a winding path of names and descriptions throughout its evolution. Even though its creator, John Holt, expressed a certain unease with the term and favored using the word 'living' instead, 'unschooling' has endured and gained widespread recognition. This broadens our understanding of the boundless possibilities encompassed within unschooling, which are as diverse and expansive as the very concept of life itself.

Holt once remarked that he found the term unsatisfactory because it primarily focuses on what unschooling is not, rather than explicitly conveying what it truly encompasses. Nevertheless, as time has marched on, the term has stood strong and maintained its relevance as the antithesis to the dominant and compulsory institution of traditional schooling.

In contemporary conversations, alternative phrases have emerged to describe similar educational approaches. Some individuals refer to it as unlearning, free-range learning, non-schooling, anti-schooling, or hack schooling, among a myriad of variations. While these alternative expressions offer unique perspectives, 'unschooling' remains the most universally recognized and commonly employed descriptor.

As the unschooling movement continues to shape itself, we must remain open to the fluidity of language and the potential for new terminology to arise. However, for the time being, 'unschooling' stands as the primary banner under which this educational philosophy gathers—a philosophy that dares to challenge the norms of traditional schooling and places emphasis on individualized, self-directed learning experiences.

The Essence of Unschooling

Unschooling, in its purest form, embodies a nurturing approach to raising children—one that embraces free play and child-directed activities to foster the development of their unique talents and boundless creativity. It is a path that wholeheartedly supports and follows the child's own interests, free from coercion, manipulation, regimentation, incessant testing and grading, hierarchical ranking, or the imposition of authoritarian rule.

To unschool a child is a departure from traditional notions of teaching, for it rejects the idea of a teacher-led or parent-led curriculum with predefined learning objectives. Instead, unschooling parents prefer to adopt the role of facilitators, learning partners who guide and support their child's educational journey. The term 'teacher' may still linger within the unschooling lexicon, a remnant of past discourses that have yet to fully embrace this transformative approach.

Unschooling stands as a beacon of liberation, liberating children from the confines of rigid structures and empowering them to explore the depths of their own innate curiosity and passion. It is a philosophy that cherishes the individuality and autonomy of each child, trusting in their natural inclination to learn and grow.

In the realm of unschooling, education becomes a fluid dance, guided by the child's own rhythm and desires. It is a dance that unfolds with love, patience, and respect, as the child's interests become the compass that steers their educational journey. Unschooling recognizes that genuine learning emerges when it is driven by intrinsic motivation and genuine interest, unburdened by external pressures or imposed objectives.

As we embrace the transformative power of unschooling, we liberate our children from the shackles of traditional schooling and embark on a remarkable voyage of discovery. In this voyage, we shed the roles of authoritarian instructors and embrace the profound joy of facilitating our children's growth, celebrating their unique brilliance and nurturing their boundless potential.

Unschooling is a revolution, a paradigm shift that challenges the status quo and breathes new life into the landscape of education. It offers a glimpse into a world where learning flourishes organically, where the pursuit of knowledge is infused with joy, and where children are honored as the architects of their own education.

The Essence of Education

Let us explore the distinction between schooling, unschooling, and true education. According to the profound insights of John Gatto, schooling is not synonymous with education; it merely entails submission to the instructions of others. Education, on the other hand, stems from real-life experiences, the environment, and the community that surrounds us. It is a natural process that thrives as long as a child's innate curiosity, intellect, and love for learning are not suppressed or mutilated by the coercive and competitive confines of the school system.

In a world where the power to dictate a child's time and activities has been seized by the political state, channeled through the bureaucratic mechanisms of School, Unschooling emerges as both a method and a philosophy. It seeks to dismantle the artificial barriers that hinder natural learning, thus creating the space for true education to flourish.

Unlike School, Unschooling is not a force imposed upon children, wherein they are taught according to the predetermined knowledge deemed essential by teachers or the State. Instead, Unschooling is a process that safeguards and nurtures a child's inherent love for learning. It is a means of ensuring that their natural inclination to explore, discover, and grow is not stifled.

Unschooling offers an alternative path, one that strives to liberate children from the confines of a rigid and prescribed curriculum. It empowers them to embrace their passions, follow their interests, and engage with the world around them in a meaningful way. Unschooling recognizes that true education blossoms when it aligns with a child's authentic desires and innate curiosity, unimpeded by external forces.

Education, at its core, transcends the confines of a traditional classroom. It is a lifelong journey of discovery, driven by the pursuit of knowledge, understanding, and personal growth. It is an endeavor that goes beyond the acquisition of facts and figures, placing emphasis on the development of critical thinking, creativity, and empathy.

In the realm of education, Unschooling stands as a beacon of hope—a means of reclaiming the freedom to learn, explore, and thrive outside the constraints of School. It is a philosophy that redefines our understanding of what it truly means to educate, shifting the focus from compliance and conformity to nurturing the natural love for learning that resides within every child's heart.

So, let us embark on this transformative journey, casting aside the limitations imposed by schooling and embracing the vast expanse of true education. Through Unschooling, we invite our children to become active participants in their own learning, to embrace their curiosity, and to embark on a lifelong adventure of growth, understanding, and self-discovery.

Unraveling the Differences

Is there a distinction between raising children and educating them? Many parents firmly believe there is. They reject the notion that the institution of School should interfere with the sacred task of nurturing, imposing a stranger to control a child's time and thoughts for an overwhelming 40 hours a week, not to mention the additional burden of homework.

Learning and education, in their purest form, are seamlessly interwoven into the tapestry of everyday life. They need not rely on an expansive and costly bureaucratic apparatus to enforce their occurrence. Instead, they naturally unfold as part of our interactions, experiences, and community engagement.

As parents, we bear the tremendous privilege and responsibility of cultivating an enriching environment for our children—a space where learning flourishes organically, unburdened by rigid structures and external pressures. We have the power to ignite their curiosity, nurture their passions, and guide their growth through genuine engagement with the world around them.

Education, in its truest essence, transcends the confines of a physical institution. It encompasses the boundless expanse of life itself—an eternal journey of exploration, comprehension, and self-actualization. Education thrives beyond the walls of a classroom; it is intricately woven into the fabric of our existence.

As we embark on this profound journey of parenting, let us cherish the belief that education is not confined to prescribed spaces or dictated by external forces. Instead, it flourishes within the loving embrace of family, community, and a world rich with opportunities for growth and knowledge.

Reclaim the power to shape our children's education, breaking free from the constraints of a system that seeks to control every aspect of their lives. Create an environment that fosters curiosity, nurtures creativity, and encourages exploration, honoring the innate thirst for knowledge that beats within every child's heart.

Trust in your ability to guide your children along their unique paths of growth and discovery. Embrace the inherent beauty of learning, recognizing it as an integral part of everyday life, with endless possibilities waiting to be explored. Together, let us cultivate a nurturing space where our children can thrive, embarking on their personal journey towards wisdom, knowledge, and fulfillment.

The Origins of Unschooling

The word "Unschooling" may initially sound negative due to its use of the prefix "un-," which often implies negation. This negative connotation can be off-putting to many individuals, as it seems to imply taking something away from a child that they had previously received. So, how does Unschooling hold any positive value or meaning?

To truly grasp the positive nature of Unschooling, one must first recognize the extent to which the traditional institution of school itself can be destructive and have negative effects. To gain a comprehensive understanding of this perspective, I recommend delving into John Taylor Gatto's enlightening work, "An Underground History of American Schooling" (2000).

John Holt (1923-1985), often regarded as the "father of the Unschooling movement," initially introduced the term. He was closely associated with Ivan Illich in the 1960s, receiving warm acknowledgments from Illich in the preface to "Deschooling Society" and in the introduction to "School is Dead" by Everett Reimer.

However, Holt's thinking gradually diverged, taking a different direction from that of Illich and Reimer. Consequently, he felt the need for a new term to distinguish his approach from theirs.

In essence, Unschooling emerges as a positive concept once we grasp the destructive and negative aspects embedded within the traditional schooling system. It signifies a departure from harmful practices and a shift towards nurturing, individualized approaches to education. Understanding the intricacies of Unschooling involves exploring the works of influential thinkers like Gatto, Holt, Illich, and Reimer, who have contributed significantly to this discourse.

By exploring these ideas, we can begin to appreciate the positive transformation that

Unschooling offers—a transformative path that honors the unique needs, interests, and passions of each child, liberating them from the confines of traditional schooling and allowing them to thrive in their pursuit of knowledge and personal growth.

Unschooling Is Not a New Idea

To what extent can we consider Unschooling a new idea? While the term itself may have emerged in the mid-1970s, the essence, practice, and phenomenon of Unschooling have deep roots that stretch back to the very inception of the concept of family. Throughout history, families have always lived and learned together, drawing knowledge and wisdom from the intricate tapestry of work, play, travel, and the vast wonders of the natural and man-made environments surrounding them.

In this light, School appears as the newcomer, the fresh-faced upstart in the educational landscape. It is the new-fangled fad that hasn't graced humanity's journey for very long. Unschooling, on the other hand, boasts a lineage that far predates the advent of formalized Schooling.

What sets Unschooling apart today is the conscious embrace and deliberate practice of this age-old tradition. Unschooling families now embark on this path with full awareness of the profound benefits it offers. Thanks to the advancements in technology, particularly the web, blogs, and social media, these families can come together, finding support and camaraderie in a community of like-minded individuals pursuing the same educational enterprise.

The power of connectivity has transformed Unschooling, allowing for the exchange of knowledge, experiences, and insights among a vast network of individuals dedicated to this alternative approach to education. While the essence of Unschooling may trace its origins back to time immemorial, this newfound awareness and the digital landscape have facilitated its resurgence and provided a platform for collective growth and learning.

So, in contemplating the novelty of Unschooling, let us recognize that it taps into an ancient wisdom, a timeless understanding of learning within the fabric of family life. Unschooling's allure lies not in its novelty but in its ability to rekindle the innate human instinct for discovery, curiosity, and self-directed growth. It invites us to embrace the timeless path of learning, liberated from the confines of conventional Schooling, and to chart our own educational journeys in harmony with the natural rhythms of life itself.

Unschooling's Strengths

The wonders of Unschooling unfold before us—a learner-centered and democratic approach to education that embraces the innate desire to learn within every child. Unschooling grants them the freedom to shape their own future, forging their own destiny.

At its core, Unschooling recognizes that learning knows no bounds. It breaks free from the confines of traditional classrooms and rigid curricula, allowing children to embark on a journey of self-discovery guided by their passions and interests. It is a profound act of love, nurturing their potential and trusting in their innate wisdom.

Unschooling trusts in our children's ability to navigate their own learning path. It acknowledges their natural curiosity and intelligence, empowering them to explore and pursue knowledge on their own terms. It is a leap of faith, an acknowledgment that as parents and educators, our role is to support and guide rather than control.

By embracing Unschooling, we provide our children with the wings to soar beyond the limitations of traditional education. We foster their creativity, critical thinking, and problem-solving skills as they immerse themselves in subjects that ignite their passions. We become facilitators and mentors, offering resources and guidance while creating an environment that nurtures curiosity and independent thinking.

The strengths of Unschooling are evident—liberation from rigid systems, affirmation of a child's innate thirst for knowledge, and a celebration of their individuality. It is an approach that values love, respect, and trust in our children's abilities. Through Unschooling, we empower them to shape their own destinies and create a future that is uniquely their own.

In the realm of Unschooling, we find the true essence of education—an exploration of the world, a cultivation of lifelong learning, and a belief in the limitless potential of our children. Let us embrace the strengths of Unschooling, honoring the extraordinary journey that awaits each young learner as they discover their place in the world and forge their own remarkable path.

Unschooling's Limitations

Just as life itself knows no bounds, Unschooling is a philosophy that thrives on the absence of limitations. It embraces the infinite possibilities and potential that reside within each child's unique journey. Yet, in the tapestry of individual lives, there are threads that weave a distinct pattern—limitations that arise in the realm of Unschooling.

Unschooling's limitations are not universal or predefined; instead, they are as diverse as the children who embark on this educational path. Each Unschooler possesses their own set of circumstances, experiences, and aspirations that shape their journey. It is within this tapestry of individuality that we find the boundaries that are unique to each child.

Just as every life has its own story, Unschooling recognizes that limitations are inherent in the human experience. While Unschooling may offer boundless opportunities for exploration and growth, it cannot replicate the exact treasures or injuries found in the lives of others. Each Unschooler walks their own path, encountering a distinct set of challenges, triumphs, and setbacks.

Rather than perceiving limitations as obstacles, Unschooling acknowledges them as integral aspects of our individuality. They are the shades that add depth to our educational journey, the intricacies that shape our understanding of the world. Unschooling invites us to embrace our limitations, recognizing that they contribute to our uniqueness and allow us to chart a path that is uniquely our own.

Learn to celebrate the limitations of Unschooling, for they are not constraints that confine us but the brushstrokes that paint a vivid portrait of our individuality. They remind us that each child's journey is a masterpiece in its own right, filled with joys, challenges, and discoveries that are as diverse as the colors of a vibrant palette. Honor the limitations that make Unschooling a deeply personal and transformative experience, unfolding the potential within each child's remarkable journey.

Chapter 2 – Embracing the Philosophy

Education Redefined

Indeed, for John Holt and the countless Unschoolers who have embraced his ideas, the verb "to Unschool" embodies the very essence of education itself. To Unschool, in their perspective, means to create an environment that nurtures learning without the necessity of traditional teaching. It is a transformative approach where the focus shifts from "schooling" or instructing to allowing and supporting the natural process of learning. In the realm of Unschooling, education flourishes organically, unfettered by the confines of conventional schooling.

To "school" implies the act of teaching or instructing, while Unschooling stands in stark contrast, emphasizing the concept of enabling and facilitating learning to unfold naturally. Unschoolers believe that traditional Schooling deliberately and detrimentally hinders this process.

This is precisely why Unschooling is regarded as a positive action—a means of unveiling, much like peeling back layers to reveal something hidden, or unharming, if such a word existed. Unschooling aims to liberate education from the restrictive structures and practices imposed by traditional schooling, fostering an environment where genuine learning can flourish.

In the absence of coercion and rigid curricula, Unschooling embraces the innate curiosity, creativity, and love for learning that resides within every child. It recognizes that true education is not confined to the walls of a classroom or dictated by external forces. Instead, it unfolds in the freedom and autonomy granted to learners, allowing them to explore, question, and make meaningful connections with the world around them.

So, yes, Unschooling is education in its purest form—a path that veers away from conventional teaching to embrace the natural process of learning. It is an act of empowerment, enabling children to embark on a journey of self-discovery, intellectual growth, and personal fulfillment. In the realm of Unschooling, education transcends the confines of schooling, becoming an exhilarating adventure that reveals the limitless potential within each learner.

Learning Through Doing

The core essence of Unschooling ultimately boils down to the idea of learning-by-doing. However, for Unschoolers, it goes beyond that simple phrase—learning is doing, and doing is learning.

In his later works, such as "Instead of Education" (1976), John Holt delved into radical territory, challenging not only the concept of education but also the very notion of learning itself. Holt argued that there is no true separation between learning and doing. They are intertwined, inseparable.

Consider learning to play the cello as an example. According to Holt, you don't embark on a process of "learning" to play the cello by merely spending a designated amount of time preparing to play it. Instead, he contends that learning and doing are one and the same. When you engage in the act of playing the cello, you are simultaneously learning and experiencing the joy and growth that comes with it. In this light, Holt questions the necessity of the term "learning" itself. If learning and doing are intricately entwined, why do we still need the word "learning" as a distinct concept?

Yet, despite these ponderings, the term "learning" persists in our vocabulary. It serves as a way to capture our understanding of the continuous growth and development that occurs through active engagement with the world.

For Unschoolers, the act of doing is not a separate entity from learning. It is through hands-on experiences, exploration, and meaningful interactions that true education takes place. Unschooling embraces the notion that knowledge is acquired, skills are honed, and wisdom is gained through the lived experience of engaging with the world around us.

In this way, Unschooling challenges the traditional compartmentalization of learning and emphasizes the holistic nature of education. It encourages individuals to fully immerse themselves in their passions, interests, and pursuits, recognizing that the journey of doing is where true learning unfolds.

Learning Through Living

For Unschoolers, the concepts of learning, living, and doing are intricately intertwined. They view them as inseparable aspects of human experience, making the term "education" redundant. According to John Holt, drawing a distinct line between education and living is impossible. Anyone who promises to "educate" you or your child is, in Holt's perspective, a deceiver or con artist seeking to exert control. Bureaucratic systems of confinement, measurement, progression, testing, and certification are unnecessary for individuals to acquire the skills and knowledge they desire.

However, there are practical challenges in completely abandoning words like "learning" and "education" because we lack a distinct alternative term to capture the idea of "the-learning-that-happens-while-doing."
Interestingly, even John Holt himself, after

emphasizing the rejection of these terms, occasionally reintroduces them in his writing. Therefore, in this book, we have chosen to continue using these words while acknowledging the reservations expressed by Holt and recognizing the complexity of the issue. Nevertheless, Holt's essential point remains valid—that the traditional understanding of education as separate from living and learning is flawed, and that true education is a natural part of the human experience.

Unschooling challenges the conventional education system by advocating for a holistic, learner-centered approach that integrates learning, living, and doing. It urges individuals to embrace their passions, follow their curiosities, and engage with the world authentically. By doing so, Unschoolers believe that individuals can acquire the knowledge, skills, and abilities they desire without relying on rigid institutional frameworks.

Unschooling or Homeschooling

When pondering the difference between Unschooling and homeschooling, it's important to recognize that homeschooling was actually the precursor to Unschooling. Before the term "Unschooling" gained prominence, homeschooling served as the initial form of this educational approach. As a result, there exists some overlap and confusion between the two, but over time, distinct differences have emerged.

Similar to Unschooling, homeschooling takes on various forms, ranging from more conventional to radical approaches, with some aligning closely with the principles of Unschooling. In many ways, homeschooling is still considered the foundation of Unschooling. However, at its core, homeschooling retains certain elements of traditional schooling. A child who is homeschooled often follows a predetermined "curriculum" composed of defined "subjects." This curriculum is typically established and monitored by a centralized authority located far away from the actual learning environment. This distance, both in geographical and imaginative terms, can create a sense of detachment, limiting the sense of responsibility and care towards the child's education.

In contrast, true Unschooling diverges from the concept of a structured curriculum and predefined subjects. It embraces a more liberated approach where learning is not confined within the boundaries of conventional subjects. Unschooling recognizes that education should not be limited by rigid guidelines but should instead foster a child's natural curiosity and passion. In a genuine Unschooling environment, learning takes shape organically, guided by the individual interests and inclinations of the learner.

While homeschooling laid the foundation for Unschooling, the essence of Unschooling lies in its rejection of curriculum-based instruction and its commitment to nurturing self-directed, holistic learning experiences. It seeks to create an educational environment where children are free to explore and learn without the constraints of predetermined subjects or external authority.

So, while homeschooling and Unschooling share historical ties, Unschooling represents a distinct evolution—a transformative approach that moves away from the confines of conventional schooling, embracing the boundless possibilities that emerge when education is driven by the individual learner's innate curiosity and genuine interests.

Closer Look at Homeschooling

Can we conclude that Unschooling surpasses homeschooling in terms of effectiveness? The answer to this question lies in the fundamental assumptions underlying standardized institutionalized schooling and the pervasive influence of the corporate state. While homeschooling may not completely break away from these assumptions, it does offer a multitude of advantages over compulsory universal schooling.

One notable distinction is the absence of physical confinement in a space that operates on surveillance and regimentation, overseen by unfamiliar figures burdened with bureaucratic constraints and mysterious codes of behavior—a labyrinth hidden from the Schooled child's understanding. In the realm of homeschooling, such confinements dissipate, replaced by an environment where children are free to explore and learn within the sanctuary of their own homes. Here, there is no pretense of an all-knowing, certified authority figure dictating orders and presenting pre-validated "truths" or information for mindless memorization and regurgitation. Instead, a guiding adult, often a parent, assumes the role of a co-explorer and a discussion partner, nurturing the child's intellectual growth.

However, perhaps the most significant advantage of homeschooling lies in the preservation of autonomy, independence, and individual identity. Unlike the suffocating compulsion experienced in the classroom, where all students are compelled to progress at the same rigid "average" pace, regardless of their unique abilities, interests, and prior knowledge of the subject matter, homeschooling celebrates the diversity of learning. It allows children to progress at their own pace, fostering a sense of autonomy and honoring their individuality. This freedom empowers learners to delve deeper into their passions, pursue topics of genuine interest, and embark on a personalized educational journey.

While homeschooling may not fully shed the shackles of traditional schooling, it presents a compelling alternative—a space where children can escape the confines of the classroom, engage in meaningful exploration alongside a supportive adult, and embrace their autonomy and individuality. It offers an opportunity for learning that aligns more closely with the child's natural rhythms, passions, and abilities—a departure from the homogenizing force of the classroom that treats every child as an average statistic.

Ultimately, the effectiveness of homeschooling, when compared to Unschooling, rests on the degree to which it breaks free from the traditional schooling paradigm, embracing the values of autonomy, individuality, and customized learning experiences.

Unschooling or Deschooling

Let's delve into the intriguing differences between Unschooling and Deschooling. Deschooling, the parent of Unschooling, laid the foundation for its more pragmatic, grounded, and practical offspring.

Deschooling emerged amidst the social turbulence of the 1960s, a period marked by profound questioning of society's core assumptions. It gained momentum from the student revolt that ignited in various corners of the world, such as Paris, UC Berkeley, and other universities during the iconic year of 1968. Deschooling, with its overtly political nature, sought to challenge the fundamental pillars of educational systems. It was a critical movement that questioned the very essence of schooling itself.

In particular, Deschooling finds its association with the influential works of Everett Reimer, known for his groundbreaking book "School is Dead," and Ivan Illich, who penned the seminal "Deschooling Society." These works emerged from their collaborations at the Centre for Intercultural Documentation in Cuernavaca, Mexico. Deschooling offered a radical critique of traditional schooling, exposing its limitations and proposing alternative visions of education.

Unschooling, on the other hand, blossomed as the pragmatic and grounded offspring of Deschooling. While Deschooling laid the ideological groundwork, Unschooling carried its principles into practical implementation. Unschooling focuses on creating real-life learning experiences that empower individuals to chart their educational paths outside the confines of traditional schooling.

While Deschooling may have been more overtly political, Unschooling shines through in its long-term effects, revolutionizing the way we think about education. Unschooling emphasizes self-directed learning, the pursuit of individual passions, and the liberation of education from rigid institutional structures.

These distinct yet interconnected movements, Deschooling and Unschooling, have played a pivotal role in reshaping our perceptions of education. They challenge the assumptions of traditional schooling, urging us to reimagine education as a dynamic and personalized journey. By embracing the ideas born from Deschooling and carried forward by Unschooling, we embark on a transformative path towards a more liberating and holistic educational landscape.

Deschooling vs. Unschooling

What sets these two approaches to School apart in practice? Let's delve into their nuances and uncover the distinctiveness that lies within.

Etymologically, the prefixes "de-" and "un-" may appear similar, with the former implying the act of taking away and the latter representing negation. Thus, Deschooling can be interpreted as "removing the concept of Schooling," while Unschooling simply signifies "not engaging in Schooling." However, their divergent contexts and usage shed light on their contrasting meanings. For instance, a deschooled society envisions a world where the institutionalized imposition of forced schooling, dictated by the corporate state, has been eradicated. On the other hand, an Unschooled child has received an education but has intentionally avoided the confines of traditional Schooling.

Here lies the crucial distinction: Deschooling pertains to the transformation of an entire society, purging it of the institution of forced schooling. It strives to challenge the stronghold of Schooling, as dictated by external entities, and seeks to remove its pervasive influence. Conversely, Unschooling acknowledges the pragmatic reality that completely abolishing Schooling on a societal level is unrealistic. Schooling is deeply entrenched within societal structures and represents an institution that society, to a large extent, embraces and expects. Instead of aiming to eradicate Schooling entirely, Unschooling embraces a more individualized approach—one child at a time—by navigating around School's negative effects and carving out alternative paths of education.

Deschooling harbors a radical intent, seeking to dismantle the very foundations of Schooling. It aspires to create a world free from its oppressive grip. Unschooling, on the other hand, acknowledges the challenges inherent in dismantling the institution of Schooling at a societal level. It recognizes that the prevailing societal desire for Schooling makes its complete eradication an impractical endeavor. Instead, Unschooling advocates for staying clear of School's limitations and detrimental impacts, prioritizing the individual's growth and education within the constraints of the existing system.

These examples showcase the divergent objectives of Deschooling and Unschooling. Deschooling aims to remove School from society entirely, while Unschooling acknowledges the prevailing reality and focuses on empowering individuals to navigate their educational journey outside the confines of traditional Schooling. Both approaches offer pathways to challenge the status quo, but in distinct ways. By understanding these differences, we gain insight into the potential for transformative change, whether on a societal level or in the lives of individual learners.

Deschoolers and Liberation

The Deschoolers were driven by a profound desire to break the chains of dependency that had bound citizens to institutions. Their mission was to restore autonomy and reclaim the essence of freedom, meticulously unraveled by the relentless expansion of impersonal and dehumanizing institutional power. For the Deschoolers, the emblematic embodiment of this encroachment was none other than the institution of School itself—an evil that had permeated society to an alarming extent, robbing individuals of their fundamental rights and freedoms.

The Deschoolers recognized that the pernicious influence of School had gone too far, depriving individuals of their agency and relegating them to passive recipients of a rigid and dehumanizing system. Their aim was to dismantle this oppressive structure, advocating for a return to small-scale, locally managed learning environments that embraced the inherent freedom and natural progression of knowledge acquisition. They envisioned a paradigm shift away from the cumbersome machinery of a centralized bureaucracy—an inefficient, costly behemoth that stifled individual growth and expression.

At the heart of their concerns was the fixed-step curriculum, an onerous apparatus that imposed conditional progression on learners. The constant testing and grading of the Schooled, an intrinsic component of the School system, acted as a tool of control, stifling creativity and curiosity. The Deschoolers challenged the notion that true expertise could be confined within the confines of certified individuals, advocating for a more organic approach to learning that freed children from the shackles of time, activity, and even physical movement for the better part of their formative years.

In essence, the Deschoolers sought to liberate society from the clutches of an overbearing institution. Their vision encompassed the restoration of individual agency, the preservation of freedom, and the rejection of a system that had subjugated learners to a predetermined and oppressive path. By unraveling the oppressive grip of School, the Deschoolers aspired to create an educational landscape that celebrated the inherent potential and innate curiosity within each individual, paving the way for a more vibrant, dynamic, and human-centered approach to learning.

Real or Radical

Within the vast realm of Unschooling, one might wonder if there exists a spectrum, a continuum that spans from ordinary Unschooling to what some might label as 'radical' Unschooling. Let's embark on a journey to uncover the nuances within this diverse landscape.

At its core, Unschooling encompasses the notion of self-directed learning intertwined with the concept of 'learning from life' itself. However, in practice, we find variations that diverge from this fundamental principle. Some individuals who identify as Unschoolers may still adhere to a strict curriculum, delivered under the authoritarian control of a parent. They might even subject their child to external test materials, enforcing a more structured and traditional approach.

While they may claim to be practicing Unschooling, it is important to recognize that this does not align with the essence of Unschooling as envisioned by its proponents. However, we must also acknowledge that there is no Unschooling Police Force, ready to enforce the 'right' way or demand conformity. Such a force could neither exist nor should it exist. Unschooling is not about conformity, but rather about celebrating the individuality and uniqueness of each learner's educational journey.

'Real' Unschooling, sometimes referred to as 'radical' Unschooling, embodies the true essence of this approach. It entails relinquishing control and allowing the child to take charge of their own learning path, with the parent/s providing support and guidance without manipulative agendas. It is a philosophy rooted in trust and respect, where the child's autonomy and curiosity are honored and nurtured.

So, within the realm of Unschooling, we find a spectrum—a range of interpretations and applications. While some may adopt a more structured approach that deviates from the core principles of Unschooling, others embrace the radical notion of empowering the child to shape their own educational agenda. By exploring this spectrum, we gain a deeper understanding of the multifaceted nature of Unschooling and the diverse ways in which it can be embraced.

Ultimately, Unschooling is a journey of self-discovery and growth, where the path taken varies from one family to another. It is a celebration of freedom, individuality, and the unwavering belief in the innate drive for learning. As we navigate this landscape, let us embrace the diversity of Unschooling and its capacity to empower learners to chart their own educational destinies.

Unschooling Beyond Marketing

Do the terms and labels we assign really make a significant difference? The answer, in the case of Unschooling, is a resounding no. While labels may serve a purpose in marketing endeavors, the essence of Unschooling transcends the need for any promotional campaigns. In fact, Unschooling stands firmly against the very notion of marketing and rejects any consumerist approach to learning.

Unschooling is a philosophy of life that defies the commodification of education. It refuses to reduce the journey of learning to a transactional process where knowledge is purchased subject by subject, akin to selecting items from the shelves of a grand education supermarket. Unschooling recognizes that learning is an inherent part of life itself—a seamless integration that permeates every aspect of our existence. It is a rejection of the idea that education can be confined to neatly framed diplomas and certificates displayed on walls. Unschooling celebrates the interconnectedness of learning and life, viewing them as inseparable entities.

The very nature of Unschooling obviates the need for formalized institutions such as an 'Institute of Unschooling' or an 'Unschooling Foundation'. To establish such organizations would be a paradox, a contradiction-in-terms. Unschooling, at its core, challenges institutionalization and the constraints it imposes on individual growth and autonomy. It thrives in the absence of rigid structures, opting for a more organic and fluid approach to education.

So, while labels may play a role in marketing and branding, the essence of Unschooling defies the need for such external trappings. Unschooling embraces a philosophy of self-directed learning and rejects the notion of education as a consumable commodity. It invites us to unravel the constraints of institutionalization and embrace the boundless potential of learning as an integral part of our lived experiences. Let us embark on this journey of Unschooling, liberated from the confines of labels, and delve into the profound possibilities that lie within the realms of self-discovery and authentic education.

Chapter 3 – Family Dynamics

Family Bonds

The impact of Unschooling on family life and the strength of family ties is a vital inquiry that delves into the very fabric of our social dynamics. Over the years, numerous sociological and psychological studies have illuminated a disheartening trend: the quality of family life and the resilience of family ties have experienced a steady decline since the aftermath of World War II. This decline can be attributed to a multitude of factors, ranging from the demands of the modern workforce to sweeping revolutions in consciousness, sexual liberation, declining birth rates, geographic mobility, urban alienation, the pervasive influence of drugs, and the prevailing trend of individual atomization within the already compact nuclear family structure.

Amidst this backdrop, Unschooling emerges as a force capable of dismantling the damaging effects that have eroded individual personal integrity within families. Some may even argue that the very aim of Unschooling is to reverse the tide, rejuvenating and fortifying the bonds that bind families together.

Unschooling operates as a catalyst for transformative change within family dynamics. By embarking on the Unschooling journey, families reclaim their autonomy, becoming active agents in shaping their own educational experiences. They step away from the societal pressures that have fractured family cohesion, and instead, they embrace a path that honors individuality, fosters genuine connections, and nurtures personal growth.

Through Unschooling, families rediscover the intrinsic value of spending time together, engaging in shared learning experiences, and celebrating the beauty of each family member's unique journey. It offers an opportunity to break free from the constraints of rigid schedules, standardized curricula, and external expectations, fostering an environment where curiosity, creativity, and exploration thrive.

By actively participating in their children's education, parents become more than mere instructors or authority figures. They become co-explorers, companions, and facilitators, forging deeper bonds with their children based on trust, mutual respect, and shared adventures in learning.

In essence, Unschooling revitalizes family life by reawakening the inherent interconnectedness of its members. It rekindles the flame of togetherness, providing a space for the nurturing of empathy, compassion, and understanding within the family unit. Through Unschooling, families find solace in the knowledge that their collective growth and well-being are paramount, laying the foundation for strong family ties that withstand the test of time.

The Sanctity of Family

The question lingers in the air: Can Unschooling truly save the family from the clutches of societal disarray? The answer remains elusive, for the forces that have wreaked havoc on family bonds are undeniably formidable. Yet, amidst this tumultuous landscape, Unschooling emerges as a beacon of hope—a movement that heralds a transformative shift in the right direction.

Unschooling holds the promise of rekindling the fading embers of familial unity and connection. It empowers those who embrace its principles, granting them the ability to navigate the terrain of family life with purpose and intentionality. The beauty of Unschooling lies in the fact that its advocates need not wait for the masses to awaken to its potential; they can forge ahead, blazing a trail of transformation within their own family units.

Unschooling offers an alternative path—one that sidesteps the confines of conventional educational systems and societal pressures. It provides families with the freedom to chart their own course, unburdened by rigid schedules, standardized curricula, and external expectations. Within the realm of Unschooling, the family unit becomes a sanctuary—a space where individuality is celebrated, and genuine connections are nurtured.

Through Unschooling, families reclaim their agency, taking active roles in their children's education and personal growth. Parents become more than mere instructors; they become guides, facilitators, and allies on the journey of lifelong learning. Unschooling affords families the opportunity to learn and explore together, forging stronger bonds and fostering a sense of shared purpose.

However, it is important to acknowledge the magnitude of the challenges that lie ahead. The destructive forces that have eroded the fabric of family life are deeply entrenched. Unschooling's ability to save the family from these perils remains to be seen, as its impact is both profound and gradual. Time will be the ultimate arbiter of Unschooling's potential to salvage the sanctity of family.

But let us not lose hope. Let us embrace the power of Unschooling as a movement in the right direction—a beacon that illuminates a path to reclaiming what has been lost. By cultivating strong family ties, fostering deep connections, and prioritizing the holistic growth of each family member, we can create a ripple effect that extends far beyond our individual households.

In the end, Unschooling offers a choice—a choice to break free from the shackles of societal norms, to prioritize family unity, and to embark on a journey of self-directed learning and discovery. Whether Unschooling can save the family in its entirety remains uncertain, but the power it holds to transform the lives of those who embrace it is undeniable.

Shifting the Focus to the Child's World

When you step into the Unschooling realm, and you'll discover a refreshing perspective that challenges traditional notions of schooling. While it may seem like a complete rejection of the school system, there are intriguing elements that bridge the gap between Unschooling and conventional education.

As we delve into Unschooling websites and engage in discussions, it's easy to see it as an anti-school movement, evoking memories of countercultural rebellions of the past. However, let me assure you that Unschooling is so much more. It revolves around engaging children in real-life activities, fostering diverse interactions with peers of varying ages and interests.

Now, here's the secret sauce of Unschooling: it transcends the confines of a prescribed curriculum. Instead, it invites us to embrace the environment as the curriculum itself—a rich tapestry of experiences, waiting to be explored. Imagine the air we breathe, the water we drink, and the vibrant life that surrounds us—all serving as the backdrop for our educational journey.

As parents who embrace the Unschooling approach, our focus shifts deliberately. We contemplate the environment we create for our children. How can we shape it to offer abundant opportunities for exploration and growth? And then, ah, here comes the pivotal moment—we step back, allowing our children to navigate their own path within this enriched environment.

Please understand that Unschooling is not a revolt against schools or adult authority. It is a conscious shift that places the child at the center of the learning experience. It celebrates the power of self-directed discovery, nurturing a deep connection between the child and the world around them.

In this remarkable paradigm, the role of the parent becomes that of a guide and facilitator, weaving threads of curiosity and exploration into the tapestry of our child's life. We embrace the child's innate drive to learn and empower them to shape their educational journey.

Don't fall into seeing Unschooling as an outright rejection of traditional schooling. Instead, recognize it as a bold reimagining—a harmonious blending of elements that work in both realms. Unschooling embraces the essence of childhood, honoring the natural thirst for knowledge and allowing our children to unfold their unique potential.

It is a dance of freedom and responsibility, where children become the architects of their own education, and parents become the steadfast supporters, guiding their steps along this remarkable journey. Unschooling invites us to embrace the beauty of individualized learning, nurturing a lifelong love for exploration and discovery in the hearts and minds of our children.

Thriving in the World of Work

When you begin thinking about employment, a question arises: How do Unschoolers navigate this terrain? Critics of Unschooling often raise concerns that these children, having grown up without rigid timetables, may struggle to adapt to the demands of the workforce. However, let me offer a different perspective, one that illuminates the remarkable capabilities of Unschoolers in the professional realm.

You see, my dear friends, Unschooling instills in children a unique skill set—the ability to choose their own paths and pursue their passions. As they step into the world of work, they do so with a deep connection to their interests and a sense of purpose. Unencumbered by external pressures and societal expectations, they gravitate toward careers that truly ignite their spirits, aligning their work with their genuine passions and innate talents.

But here's the captivating aspect—Unschooling goes beyond academic pursuits. It prepares children for the realities of the real world. By engaging with life outside the classroom, Unschoolers come face-to-face with rules, responsibilities, and the understanding that the world does not revolve around them. They learn the importance of chores, of fulfilling obligations, and of adapting to different environments.

Thus, far from being ill-prepared, Unschoolers possess a unique perspective. They understand how they fit into the world, appreciating the value of collaboration, adaptability, and lifelong learning. Rather than conforming to rigid structures, they embrace the freedom to explore, innovate, and make meaningful contributions in their chosen fields.

So, when Unschoolers embark on their professional journeys, they bring with them a wealth of self-awareness, resilience, and a genuine passion for their work. They navigate the ever-changing landscape of the workforce with a spirit of curiosity and a thirst for continuous growth.

Never underestimate the power of Unschooling in shaping confident, adaptable individuals ready to make their mark in the world of work. Unschoolers are not bound by timetables, but instead are driven by purpose, carving their own unique paths and flourishing in realms where passion and purpose intersect.

Balancing Through Life's Hoops

The path of Unschooling is a unique educational journey, one that challenges the conventions of traditional schooling. As parents, we embark on the task of finding a delicate equilibrium—a balance between embracing the freedom of Unschooling and equipping our children with the skills they need to thrive in a world that may not align with their unconventional learning approach.

Within the realm of Unschooling, each family becomes the architect of their own educational framework. We craft rules and guidelines that foster our children's growth and development, instilling values, manners, and practical life tasks that extend beyond the confines of a traditional school. Simple acts like writing thank-you notes to express gratitude teach our children the importance of consideration and appreciation.

Although Unschooling may not present the same structured hoops as traditional schools, it does not leave our children ill-prepared for the real world. In fact, Unschooling offers them a distinct advantage—the opportunity to engage with the world itself. Through authentic experiences and interactions with a diverse range of individuals, our children naturally encounter the challenges and hurdles that exist beyond the classroom walls.

These real-world hoops come in various forms—managing personal finances, solving everyday problems, and honing effective communication skills. In the realm of Unschooling, our children become active participants in their own education, immersing themselves in the ebb and flow of the world around them. They learn to adapt, explore, and discover their place within the intricate tapestry of society.

Unschooling equips our children with a different set of tools—a repertoire of self-directed learning, critical thinking, and resourcefulness. Rather than adhering to a rigid curriculum, they are empowered to embrace curiosity, pursue their passions, and forge their own unique paths in life.

As parents, we play a crucial role in guiding our children through the delicate dance between Unschooling and the demands of the world. We offer gentle guidance, expanding their horizons with insights and perspectives. We nurture their social-emotional development, instilling empathy, respect, and the value of collaboration.

The key to success lies in finding harmony between the principles of Unschooling and the practical realities of life. It is a delicate balancing act, honoring our children's individuality and autonomy while providing the necessary support to navigate the diverse challenges they may encounter.

So, fellow seekers of educational freedom, let us embrace the absence of traditional hoops in the Unschooling journey. Instead, let us celebrate the vast opportunities for growth and exploration that lie before us. Together, let us equip our children with the tools to leap through life's hurdles, whether they are provided by society or self-created. As we navigate this path, we weave the perfect blend of Unschooling and life's rich tapestry, fostering a love of learning and a boundless spirit of discovery within our children's hearts.

Embracing Life's Unpredictability

Within the realm of Unschooling, the concept of "going wrong" takes on a different hue. You see, Unschooling is intricately woven into the fabric of life itself. Therefore, any challenges that arise are intertwined with the circumstances and experiences that encompass the child's world. It is in these moments that Unschooling truly reveals its resilience and adaptability.

Life, as we know it, is unpredictable. It throws us curveballs when we least expect them. A parent falling ill or passing away, a family facing financial adversity due to a stock market crash, or the distressing circumstances surrounding a relative's legal troubles—these are the realities that may shape the Unschooling journey.

Yet, even in the face of such adversities, Unschooling remains rooted in the essence of life. It is not confined to the realm of textbooks or structured lessons. Instead, it embraces the entirety of human experience. Each twist and turn becomes an opportunity for exploration and understanding.

In the realm of Unschooling, there is no notion of learning gone awry. Even the most somber or disconcerting events can serve as catalysts for growth and learning. They become poignant subjects for study, inviting deep reflection and meaningful insights.

Unschooling encompasses the fluidity and adaptability that life demands. It teaches us to embrace the ebb and flow of existence, to find value in every circumstance, and to harness the power of resilience when faced with adversity.

So, when challenges arise within the Unschooling journey, remember that they are not setbacks, but rather opportunities for growth and exploration. Unschooling thrives amidst the unpredictability of life, offering a pathway where even the darkest moments can illuminate profound understanding and resilience.

Chapter 4 – Learning

The Essence of "Real Learning"

The notion of "real learning" brings to mind the work of Charles Murray, a conservative libertarian commentator who explored the topic in his book, *Real Education: Four Simple Truths for Bringing America's Schools Back to Reality* (2008).

Murray's focus lies on the upper echelons of academic performance, often referred to as the "gifted and talented." He argues for a more efficient allocation of resources within the schooling system, ensuring that these academically exceptional students receive the education they deserve. His concern revolves around optimizing the education of this elite group, rather than challenging the institution of schooling itself.

In this context, "real learning" becomes an exclusive concept, reserved for the intellectual elite. According to Murray, the learning experiences of the lower classes are deemed unreal or insignificant. It is through this lens that he criticizes initiatives like the US Congress's "No Child Left Behind" Act (2002), arguing that it naively assumes that legislation alone can guarantee equal ability and academic success for all children.

While Murray's critique of the "No Child Left Behind" Act may hold merit, it is important to note that his perspective diverges greatly from the democratic and egalitarian principles embraced by the Unschooling movement. Unschooling, rooted in libertarianism, advocates for a holistic approach to education that values every individual's unique talents and abilities. It rejects the notion of elitism, instead aiming to empower all children to flourish and succeed.

In the realm of "real learning," Murray's libertarian elitism contrasts sharply with the democratic ideals of Unschooling. Unschooling seeks to nurture the innate curiosity and potential within every child, offering an alternative to the narrow confines of traditional schooling. It rejects the notion that only a select few are worthy of "real learning," instead championing an inclusive and egalitarian approach that celebrates the diverse abilities and aspirations of all children.

While the concept of "real learning" may carry different connotations for various perspectives, it is essential to recognize the importance of fostering a learning environment that respects and nurtures the potential within every individual. True education should be a transformative journey, accessible to all, and free from the limitations imposed by elitist ideologies.

The Joy of Immersion

Behold the wonders of intellectual curiosity! It burns brightly within the hearts of children, propelling them to seek knowledge and explore the world. Yet, within the confines of traditional schooling, the boundaries of curricula often fail to align with their true passions and interests. But fear not, for Unschooling is here—a dynamic approach that empowers children to delve into topics that ignite their curiosity and captivate their minds.

In the realm of history, Unschoolers shine with fervor. They recognize its significance, understanding that to navigate the present and shape the future, one must first understand the past. The Civil War or World War II? These are not mere chapters to be memorized and forgotten. No, they are captivating narratives that Unschoolers approach with genuine interest and engagement.

Unlike their peers in traditional classrooms, Unschooler students are free from the fear of forgetting facts or enduring exams. They embrace the opportunity to immerse themselves in the rich tapestry of historical events, delving deep into the stories, exploring causes and effects, and drawing connections to the world around them.

Immerse yourself in the beauty of Unschooling, where boundaries between disciplines blur and intertwine. Imagine the wonders of learning blocks, where subjects like Egypt come alive. Math and geometry measure the grandeur of pyramids, while Social Studies unveils the vibrant tapestry of Egyptian culture. Science takes them on a journey to understand papyrus and the art of papermaking. Art becomes a gateway to recreate the beauty of hieroglyphics, allowing their creativity to flourish.

This immersion fosters a deep connection between the child and the subject at hand. It sparks a fire within their souls, igniting a lifelong passion for learning and discovery.

So, let us celebrate the joy of immersion that Unschooling brings. Let us embrace the freedom to explore the topics that captivate our minds and nourish our intellectual growth. Together, we delve into the annals of history, uncovering the wisdom of the past and weaving it into the fabric of our present and future.

In the realm of Unschooling, knowledge knows no bounds. It is a journey that celebrates the innate curiosity of children, allowing them to follow their passions and develop a deep understanding of the world. Through this dynamic approach, Unschoolers unlock the treasures of history, discovering the threads that connect us all and shaping a brighter tomorrow.

The Power of Genuine Learning

What sets Unschooler kids on a path of remarkable progress in their learning, surpassing their Schooled counterparts? The answer lies in the inefficiencies that plague the traditional schooling system—inefficiencies that Unschooling deftly sidesteps.

In the realm of traditional schooling, a significant portion of time is lost in non-essential activities. Attendance checks, disciplinary measures, and homework monitoring consume a staggering 40 to 50% of the school day. Such unproductive time-uses hinder the true purpose of education—learning and growth.

Furthermore, the classroom dynamic often forces teachers to split their attention, catering to the needs of slower learners while simultaneously challenging those who are ahead of their peers. This juggling act diverts valuable time and attention away from actual learning, creating an inefficient environment that impedes academic progress.

But here's where Unschooling shines with its inherent advantage— genuine interest-driven learning. Unschoolers are not subjected to the compulsion that stifles natural curiosity and hampers intellectual growth. Instead, they are free to explore subjects and delve into areas that pique their curiosity and ignite their passion.

Unschooling recognizes that true learning occurs when individuals are driven by their own intrinsic motivation. By embracing their interests and following their natural curiosities, Unschooler kids tap into a wellspring of enthusiasm that propels them on a transformative learning journey.

The inefficiencies and constraints of traditional schooling pale in comparison to the boundless potential of Unschooling. With its focus on genuine interest and self-directed learning, Unschooling unleashes the true power of education, enabling children to thrive and progress at their own pace.

Embrace the freedom to learn authentically, unshackled from the limitations of compulsory education. Unschooling empowers children to become active participants in their own education, fueling their innate curiosity and propelling them towards remarkable academic achievement.

Unlocking the Joy of Learning

One of the beautiful aspects of Unschooling is that it honors the natural curiosity and intrinsic motivation of children. As a parent, you don't have to resort to forcing or cajoling your child to learn. In fact, attempting to do so can have the opposite effect, stifling their enthusiasm and dampening their natural love for learning.

Children are innately eager to explore, discover, and develop themselves. They possess an abundance of energy and an insatiable thirst for knowledge. Your role as a parent-teacher is not to impose learning upon them, but rather to be a source of interest and support as they embark on their learning journey.

Instead of trying to force-feed information, embrace the role of a facilitator, guiding your child and providing them with the resources they need to pursue their interests. Encourage their curiosity, engage in meaningful conversations, and help them access the tools and materials that ignite their passion.

By fostering an environment of support and genuine interest, you create a space where your child feels empowered and motivated to explore their learning interests. This intrinsic motivation is the driving force behind their educational growth and ensures that the learning process remains joyful and fulfilling.

Remember, your child is not lazy. They are simply waiting for the right environment to unleash their natural love for learning. So, instead of resorting to force, embrace the role of a compassionate guide, nurturing their curiosity and creating opportunities for them to thrive. Together, you will embark on a journey of discovery, unlocking the endless wonders of knowledge and nurturing a lifelong love for learning.

Curiosity and Exploration

As the golden rays of dawn peek through the curtains, the Unschooler child awakens with a sense of excitement and curiosity, eager to embark on a day of limitless possibilities. The rhythm of their day is not dictated by bells or rigid schedules, but rather by their own inner compass, guiding them towards knowledge, creativity, and self-discovery.

With the world as their classroom, breakfast becomes a gateway to scientific inquiry. In the kitchen, armed with ingredients and a spirit of adventure, they set out to create a soufflé. As the delicate mixture rises and transforms, they ponder the chemical reactions occurring between milk and eggs. A spark of curiosity ignites within them, and they venture into the realm of online research, exploring the intricacies of this culinary alchemy.

With their appetite for knowledge satiated, it's time for another culinary experiment. The Unschooler child dives back into the kitchen, armed with newfound insights. They tweak the ingredients, carefully noting the subtle differences that arise in their second soufflé creation. Through this playful exploration, they not only hone their culinary skills but also sharpen their observational acumen, becoming attuned to the nuances of flavor and texture.

In the afternoon, the Unschooler child embraces the opportunity to engage with the wider community. They attend a Spanish class at a local community college, immersing themselves in a new language and culture. The classroom becomes a vibrant melting pot of ideas, where they connect with peers and expand their linguistic horizons.

Afterward, nature beckons. They embark on a tranquil hike, guided by the call of a bird's nest they had observed being meticulously crafted by a robin. In the embrace of nature's serenity, they witness the beauty of life unfolding and deepen their connection with the natural world.

As evening descends, they retreat to the world of literature. With a captivating novel in hand, they delve into its pages, transported to faraway lands and enchanted by the power of storytelling. Compelled to share their insights, they take to their blog, weaving words with thoughtfulness and eloquence, sparking conversations and inviting others to embark on their literary journey.

With the day drawing to a close, the Unschooler child rests their head on the pillow, filled with a profound sense of fulfillment and anticipation for the adventures that tomorrow will bring. Each day is a tapestry woven with threads of curiosity, discovery, and personal growth, unique to the individual Unschooler and their family.

But remember, that the Unschooler's day is as diverse as the stars in the night sky. It is shaped by the distinct passions, interests, and opportunities that flow through each child's life. To truly grasp the intricacies of an Unschooler's day, I invite you to delve into the writings of Unschooling families, explore the captivating websites and blogs created by unschooled children themselves. Through these narratives, you will uncover a rich mosaic of experiences that illuminate the beauty and boundless potential of the Unschooling journey.

Self-Discovery in Unschooling

Step into the realm of another Unschooler's day, where the path unfolds in unexpected ways and individuality reigns supreme. While each Unschooler's journey is as unique as a fingerprint, let me paint a picture of another extraordinary day in this realm of self-directed learning.

As the morning sun stretches across the horizon, the Unschooler child arises at their own rhythm, unfettered by the constraints of a rigid schedule. Embracing the freedom that Unschooling affords, they leisurely enjoy a bowl of their favorite cereal, savoring the simplicity of their morning ritual.

With breakfast complete, the day's adventures begin. They dive headfirst into a captivating video game, immersing themselves in a digital realm that challenges their strategic thinking, dexterity, and problem-solving skills. The game becomes a canvas for their imagination, a realm where they strive to surpass their previous achievements and conquer new frontiers.

As the hours tick by, their passion for the game remains unyielding. Determined to outdo their own score and push the boundaries of their abilities, they engage in focused gameplay, honing their reflexes and sharpening their cognitive agility.

Yet, in the ebb and flow of their day, a desire for variety beckons. They momentarily set aside the console and satisfy their appetite with a simple sandwich for lunch. A brief respite renews their energy, and with curiosity as their compass, they embark on a search for new experiences.

The television screen flickers to life, offering a gateway to the world beyond. However, even the allure of the screen eventually wanes, for the Unschooler craves a deeper connection with knowledge, seeking a personal path of discovery.

Returning to their beloved video game, they gradually find satisfaction in their accomplishments. A sense of fulfillment fills their being, and they turn their attention to other avenues of learning. It could be a thought-provoking conversation with a family member, a dive into a thought-provoking book, or a venture into the boundless realm of the internet.

The beauty of Unschooling lies in its rejection of predefined expectations, allowing the Unschooler to follow their own internal compass. This philosophy is not about abandoning education but rather about unlocking the innate desire for knowledge and fostering a lifelong passion for learning.

While society may sometimes question or misunderstand Unschooling, the Unschooler remains steadfast in their pursuit of authentic education. Unschooling represents a vibrant subcategory of homeschooling, a dynamic movement that shatters the limitations imposed by rigid curricula and age-based expectations. It liberates the individual, enabling them to delve into their passions, explore their interests, and forge their own educational path.

So, whether your day is filled with digital conquests, literary escapades, or captivating discussions, embrace the essence of Unschooling—a journey of self-discovery, fueled by inner motivation and a thirst for knowledge. Open your mind to the possibilities that lie beyond conventional norms and let the beauty of Unschooling unfold in your own extraordinary day.

Nurturing Curiosity

As an Unschooling parent, the organization of work for my children takes on a unique and fluid approach. When my little ones display a spark of interest in a particular subject or topic, it ignites a fire within me to provide them with the tools and resources they need to delve deeper into their curiosity. In this realm, the child's interest becomes our curriculum, and the home transforms into their school.

For many of us, the journey into Unschooling begins with a book that resonates deep within our souls—John Holt's masterpiece, *How Children Learn*. Its pages unlock a world of possibilities, where learning revolves around the child's passions and abilities. We are captivated by the notion that education can be an organic extension of our parenting, seamlessly intertwining with the natural rhythm of our lives.

In my case, Unschooling unfolded effortlessly as I embraced a parenting style that embraced following my children's lead. I became their steadfast companion, accompanying them on their journey of discovery and growth. I observed their interests, listened to their questions, and eagerly sought out avenues to nurture their innate love of learning.

But how does the work take shape in our Unschooling household? It begins with keen observation, attuned to the flicker of curiosity that sparks within my child's eyes. Once identified, I immerse myself in the role of facilitator, meticulously curating an environment brimming with resources, experiences, and opportunities that align with their interests.

Whether it's providing a stack of books on marine biology for my budding marine enthusiast or connecting them with a local artist for immersive art sessions, I strive to fuel their passions and kindle the flames of their intellectual growth. Through these tailored experiences, my children become active participants in their own education, charting their unique course of exploration.

But let me be clear—it's not a one-size-fits-all approach. Unschooling embraces the individuality of each child, recognizing that their journey of discovery is as unique as their fingerprints. It's a dance of adaptability and flexibility, as we navigate uncharted territories hand in hand.

In our Unschooling home, learning intertwines seamlessly with life itself. As we cook together, we explore the wonders of science and mathematics. A simple walk through nature becomes an immersive lesson in ecology, as we marvel at the interconnectedness of the world around us. We find inspiration in the arts, history, and the vast expanse of human knowledge, weaving these threads into the tapestry of our everyday existence.

Yet, amidst this freedom and self-directed exploration, there is a constant undercurrent— a deep commitment to instilling values, fostering empathy, and nurturing their social-emotional well-being. We cultivate an environment that embraces respect, collaboration, and an unwavering sense of responsibility for oneself and others.

The work we undertake is not confined to textbooks and rigid schedules. It is an ever-evolving dance of inspiration, discovery, and intentional guidance. It is the art of molding an environment that sparks the flames of curiosity, fostering a love for lifelong learning, and shaping individuals who are ready to embrace the boundless possibilities that await them.

In this grand tapestry of Unschooling, we celebrate the individuality of each child, honoring their passions and unique paths of growth. It is a journey filled with joy, challenges, and countless moments of wonder. Together, we embark on this adventure, carving out a world where education transcends boundaries and where our children's dreams and aspirations can soar to unimaginable heights.

Nurturing Lifelong Adaptability

As a parent navigating the realm of Unschooling, you may find yourself pondering a pressing question: Will my Unschooled child acquire the essential skills needed for their future life and career? Let us embark on a journey of exploration and discovery to uncover the profound impact of Unschooling on their path to success.

In truth, the future is a vast and uncertain landscape, a tapestry yet to be woven. Neither you nor I can predict with certainty what lies ahead for your child—their life, their career, their unique journey. But here's the remarkable truth: institutional public schools are no fortune-tellers either.

Schools, bound by fixed curricula and rigid structures, cannot foresee the world that awaits in the next five years, nor can they anticipate the jobs that will emerge. Their constraints mirror the limitations of our own predictive abilities. However, by embracing the principles of Unschooling, you are bestowing upon your child a precious gift—the preservation of their innate and boundless love for learning.

Unschooling fosters a lifelong connection to the joy of discovery. It safeguards the flame of curiosity, igniting an insatiable thirst for knowledge within your child's heart. In doing so, it equips them with a powerful advantage—the ability to adapt to an ever-changing future with grace and agility.

While traditional schooling may inadvertently crush a child's love of learning under the weight of conformity and rigid standards, Unschooling nurtures and preserves that sacred flame. It fosters an environment where learning flourishes organically, unbound by prescribed timelines or predetermined outcomes.

Through Unschooling, your child becomes an active participant in shaping their educational journey. They engage with the world around them, immersing themselves in experiences that spark their curiosity and fuel their passion. They learn the art of self-directed exploration, acquiring not only knowledge but also invaluable skills such as critical thinking, adaptability, and a relentless hunger for growth.

In this dynamic landscape of Unschooling, your child cultivates the very qualities that will enable them to navigate an ever-evolving world with confidence and resilience. Their innate love of learning becomes a compass, guiding them through uncharted territories, and empowering them to thrive amidst change.

So fear not for your child's future. Embrace the liberating power of Unschooling and unleash the full potential that lies within. By safeguarding their love of learning, you equip them with the tools needed to conquer the challenges of tomorrow. Allow yourself to celebrate the unfolding journey, knowing that through Unschooling, your child possesses the resiliency and adaptability to shape their own destiny.

Nurturing the Learning Spirit

Remind yourself the only constant is change. Unschooling is where the ebb and flow of learning intertwines with the rhythms of your child's growth. Yet, amidst this journey, you may encounter a familiar question: What if my child resists the Unschooling mode of learning? Fear not, for every twist and turn in the path holds an opportunity for understanding and growth.

In Unschooling, we embrace the inherent curiosity and thirst for knowledge that resides within every child's heart. It is a fundamental truth that all children possess a natural inclination to learn. However, the timing and receptivity to certain subjects or concepts may vary from one child to another.

If your child seems resistant to a particular mode of learning in the Unschooling approach, it is not a sign of failure or cause for concern. Rather, it is an invitation to explore new avenues, to adapt our approach, and to discover the methods that resonate with their current state of readiness.

Just as a skilled navigator adjusts their course to navigate changing tides, we, as Unschooling parents, must navigate the ever-changing landscape of our child's learning journey. We must become relentless seekers, seeking out different avenues and paths that ignite the spark of curiosity within them.

Observe your child closely, for their resistance may reveal a misalignment between the mode of learning and their current developmental stage. It is not a matter of forcing or coercing, but of patiently seeking the right avenues that will unlock their innate desire to learn.

Unschooling celebrates the diversity of learning experiences and recognizes that there is no one-size-fits-all approach. It is a tapestry woven with countless threads of exploration and discovery. As we embark on this voyage together, we must be open to experimentation, embracing the beauty of trial and error, until we find the perfect harmony between their readiness and the methods that inspire them.

Remember that every child's learning journey is unique, and patience is the compass that guides us. Stay attuned to their changing needs and interests and persist in your search for the right pathway to ignite their learning spirit.

The refusal to learn simply signifies that the timing is not yet aligned with the subject at hand. It is an invitation to delve deeper, to listen intently, and to unlock the hidden doorways that will lead to their profound engagement and understanding.

You'll have to learn to embrace the dance of adaptation and perseverance; to navigate the tides of resistance with unwavering determination, knowing that within each challenge lies an opportunity for growth for you, the parent, as well. Through patience, creativity, and an unwavering belief in your child's innate love for learning, you will unlock the doors to a world of boundless possibilities in the realm of Unschooling.

Embracing the Uncharted Path

The world of Unschooling is a fascinating and enigmatic realm, where the boundaries are fluid and the statistics elusive. When it comes to the number of children who are Unschooled or homeschooled, we find ourselves in uncharted territory.

Unlike traditional schooling, which is meticulously recorded and tracked, homeschooling exists largely under the radar, making it challenging to determine the exact figures. However, amidst the ambiguity, glimpses of insight emerge. An article in the New York Times ventured to estimate that approximately 3% of U.S. students are engaged in the world of Unschooling.

Yet, even this estimation only scratches the surface of the vast landscape of homeschooling. Some sources suggest that the numbers could range from 1 million to 2 million children in the United States who are pursuing education outside the confines of a traditional school.

However, as we delve deeper into the intricacies of the Unschooling movement, we encounter an intriguing dilemma—the line between homeschooling and Unschooling remains fluid and undefined. The true extent of Unschoolers within the broader homeschooling community remains a mystery, as the distinction between the two approaches blurs and evolves.

As you embark on this unconventional educational journey, embrace the unknown and celebrate the diversity that thrives within the realm of Unschooling. Though the exact figures may elude you, the impact of this educational path resonates deeply with those who dare to embrace the freedom of learning beyond the traditional confines. Allow yourself to venture into uncharted territory, guided by the belief that education is a boundless adventure awaiting exploration.

The Freedom to Learn

What do those who have walked the path of Unschooling say is its greatest gift? It's the fostering of curiosity—the driving force behind the pursuit of knowledge. Unschoolers have the freedom to follow their innate curiosity, diving deep into the subjects that captivate their minds. And when they step into the world of college, they quickly realize that this sense of curiosity sets them apart from their peers.

One advocate of Unschooling, Sandra Dodd, paints a vivid picture of an Unschooler's day— a day that feels like the best Saturday you could ever dream of. Dodd, a mother who unschooled her three grown children, never doubted that they would learn math, language, and storytelling, even though these subjects were never formally "taught." She has unwavering faith in the power of natural learning, the notion that you can only truly learn that which ignites your interest. For Dodd, Unschooling is about creating and nurturing an environment where this natural learning can flourish.

The true beauty of being an Unschooler lies in the freedom to make one's own decisions and discoveries. Unschoolers take on the responsibility of managing their time, crafting their own schedules, and shaping their own lives. It's a path of self-determination and empowerment, where children learn the value of autonomy and accountability.

In the realm of Unschooling, the possibilities are boundless. Children have the agency to pursue their passions, explore their interests, and uncover the depths of their potential. They are not confined by rigid structures or predetermined paths. Instead, they embark on a journey of self-discovery, guided by their natural curiosity and the rich tapestry of life itself.

Unschooling offers a paradigm shift—an invitation to embrace the joy of learning, fueled by personal interest and genuine enthusiasm. It nurtures a deep connection between the learner and the subject matter, cultivating a lifelong love for exploration and discovery.

So, if you find yourself drawn to the allure of Unschooling, remember the gift it bestows— the freedom to follow your curiosity, to chart your own course, and to unearth the treasures that lie within. Embrace the responsibility that comes with this journey, and revel in the endless possibilities that unfold when you dare to step outside the confines of traditional education. Unschooling beckons, offering you the chance to shape your own destiny and embark on an extraordinary voyage of self-directed learning.

The Value of Rote-Learning

Rote learning refers to the memorization and repetition of information or skills through mechanical repetition without a deep understanding of the underlying concepts. It involves learning through repetition, often involving the recitation or copying of information or the practice of specific tasks until they become automatic.

In rote learning, the emphasis is placed on memorizing facts, formulas, vocabulary, or sequences without necessarily comprehending the meaning or context behind them. This method has been widely used in traditional educational systems, where students are expected to memorize and reproduce information accurately, often through drills and repetitive exercises.

While rote learning can be effective for acquiring certain types of knowledge or skills, such as multiplication tables or spelling words, critics argue that it often lacks deeper understanding, critical thinking, and the ability to apply knowledge in different contexts. The focus on memorization alone may hinder creativity, problem-solving skills, and the development of a holistic understanding of a subject.

In recent years, there has been a shift towards more experiential and inquiry-based learning approaches, which prioritize understanding, critical thinking, and application of knowledge. However, some proponents of rote learning argue that it can still have value in certain contexts, such as when foundational knowledge or basic skills need to be mastered before higher-level thinking can occur.

Ultimately, the effectiveness and appropriateness of rote learning depend on the learning objectives, the subject matter, and the individual learner's preferences and needs.

Contrary to popular belief, Unschoolers hold the older practice of rote-learning in high regard, considering it far superior to the diluted and simplified approach adopted by mainstream education. The abandonment of drills and memorization tasks in the name of making School easier has, in fact, led to the intellectual stagnation and underestimation of students' abilities.

Rote-learning, when properly utilized, becomes a catalyst for a child's growth and self-empowerment. It provides a solid foundation and strengthens their cognitive capabilities in ways that the modern educational system fails to achieve.

Renowned educator John Gatto passionately criticizes the school system of the past century precisely because it failed to challenge students and deprived them of demanding tasks. Instead of treating them as capable individuals, schools treated them as intellectual inferiors. In contrast, John Holt praises the 'old-school' approach to learning, particularly highlighting the Spanish language classes taught at CIDOC in Cuernavaca. These classes exemplify the value of rigorous and focused learning methods.

In the Unschooling world, the significance of rote-learning is not dismissed. It is seen as an effective tool for building knowledge, enhancing memory, and fostering intellectual growth. Unschoolers recognize that the right balance of challenging tasks, including drills and memorization, can empower children and enable them to reach their full potential.

Chapter 5 – Schooling

Challenging the Notion of School

Have we, perhaps, been too quick to associate School with the fundamental principles of democracy? The Deschoolers had a different perspective on this matter—an insight that prompts us to reexamine our assumptions.

To the Deschoolers, the very nature of compulsory education, where non-attendance is met with legal punishment, spoke volumes about its anti-democratic essence. Anything we are coerced to do, an endeavor that seeks to homogenize individuals through centrally imposed policies, bears a striking resemblance to the methods of command-and-control employed in communist regimes. Yet, the Deschoolers' critique extended beyond School itself, encompassing a broader scrutiny of institutions. In the words of Ivan Illich:

"The right of free assembly has been politically recognized and culturally accepted.

We should now understand that this right is curtailed by laws that make some forms of assembly obligatory. This is especially the case with institutions which conscript according to age group, class, or sex, and which are very time-consuming. The army is one example. School is an even more outrageous one."

For the Deschoolers, School served as a microcosm—a model that reflected the workings of all institutions. Their vision of Deschooling aimed to dismantle the pervasive institutionalization that permeated society and the lives of individuals. It was a grand endeavor that went beyond the boundaries of Unschooling, which focused on proposing and practicing alternative approaches to learning, bypassing or eluding the traditional schooling system. Unschooling, while content to pave its own path and explore new horizons, entrusted the wider social and political consequences of its work to unfold naturally.

The Deschoolers' critique of School encompassed a deep understanding of institutionalization as a whole, urging us to reconsider our societal structures and the impact they have on individual freedom and autonomy. By challenging the compulsory and oppressive nature of School and advocating for the liberation of individuals from institutional constraints, the Deschoolers beckoned us to envision a society where institutionalization yields to the flourishing of human potential and the embrace of diverse paths to learning and growth.

The Traditional School System

What do the most Unschoolers' parents think about the mainstream schools? Allow me to shed light on the profound insights and perspectives that reside within the minds of these parents. They have a unique vantage point, a perspective that challenges the very foundations of the traditional school system.

Even the best school districts, in the eyes of Unschooling parents, find themselves constrained by bureaucratic red tape and a one-size-fits-all approach that prioritizes managing numbers rather than nurturing the individual child's education. It is within this system that many students lack access to appropriate materials and fail to receive the individual attention they truly need. Unschooling parents recognize that each child is unique, with distinct needs and learning styles that deserve personalized attention.

Moreover, Unschooling parents perceive a fundamental flaw in the school system's approach to learning. They believe that students are forced to conform to a predetermined curriculum, dictated by what the school deems important. In stark contrast, Unschoolers revel in the freedom to pursue their passions, to delve deeply into subjects that ignite their curiosity and keep the flame of learning burning bright. By following their own interests, Unschoolers embark on a journey of self-discovery and intellectual growth.

Furthermore, Unschooling parents contend that the traditional school model, with its reliance on textbooks and rigid teaching protocols, is outdated in our rapidly advancing technological age. The world is evolving at an unprecedented pace, with new information, discoveries, and studies emerging faster than the school system can update its textbooks. Unschooling parents advocate for an education that embraces the dynamic nature of knowledge, where learning is not confined to static texts but rather thrives in the exploration of diverse resources and real-life experiences.

For many Unschooling parents, the traditional school system feels antiquated, ill-suited for the demands of the new age we are living in. They yearn for an educational paradigm that celebrates individuality, fosters a love for learning, and adapts to the ever-changing landscape of knowledge and innovation. It is through Unschooling, they believe, that their children can truly flourish and navigate the complexities of the modern world.

Social Engineering

The ongoing battle between Unschooling and social engineering is a clash of contrasting ideologies, each vying for control over the educational landscape. Unschoolers passionately advocate for a more organic and individualized approach to learning, emphasizing the importance of self-directed education and freedom from the dictates of the political state. They argue that education should be a personal journey, shaped by the unique interests, strengths, and curiosities of each child.

On the other hand, social engineering through the institution of Schooling aligns with the belief that education should serve broader societal goals. It is seen as a means to shape and mold the younger generation into a predetermined mold that fits societal norms and expectations. The political state often wields this influence to enforce standardized curricula, uniform assessments, and a predetermined set of knowledge and values.

The Unschoolers challenge this top-down approach, questioning the effectiveness and fairness of a system that prioritizes conformity over individual growth. They believe that children are naturally curious, capable of pursuing their own interests and passions, and that true learning occurs when individuals have the freedom to explore and discover at their own pace.

Despite the strong arguments put forth by the Unschoolers, the political state maintains its firm grip on the institution of Schooling. It sees education as a means to exert control, shape societal narratives, and maintain a sense of order and conformity. The political elite, entrenched in their positions of power, show little inclination to challenge the status quo or consider alternative educational paradigms.

However, the Unschooling movement continues to gain momentum and support, fueled by a growing number of parents and educators who are dissatisfied with the current system. As more individuals recognize the limitations of traditional schooling and embrace the principles of Unschooling, the pressure on the political state to reevaluate its approach to education may intensify.

The future of Unschooling and the role of the political state in education remain uncertain. It is an ongoing struggle, characterized by a clash of ideals and visions for the future. Only time will reveal whether the pendulum will swing towards a more liberated and personalized approach to learning, or if the forces of social engineering will maintain their stronghold.

Socialization

The question that never fails to make Unschoolers roll their eyes is the one concerning socialization of their children. Critics argue that the lack of connection with same-age peers adversely impacts the development of Unschooled kids. They claim that traditional schools, with their age-segregated classrooms and limited adult-child ratio, better prepare children for the real world. However, Unschoolers and their parent-teachers have a different perspective.

For most Unschoolers, socialization is not just a box to check—it's a vital aspect of their educational journey. They believe in genuine human connections, fostering relationships that transcend age, wealth, power, and social status. Rather than confining their children to the narrow confines of same-age interactions, Unschooling parents encourage them to engage with individuals from all walks of life.

And here's the intriguing twist—Unschooled children acquire socialization skills a hundred times more effectively outside the walls of a traditional school. They thrive in the real-life setting, where every person they meet becomes a teacher, imparting invaluable lessons about life. From the grocery store clerk sharing stories about their hometown to the elderly neighbor recounting tales of wisdom, Unschoolers encounter people of all ages and backgrounds throughout their day.

The beauty of this unconventional approach is that Unschoolers navigate a diverse tapestry of human interactions. They learn to communicate and collaborate with individuals from various cultures, professions, and life experiences. By engaging with a rich mosaic of perspectives, Unschoolers develop empathy, understanding, and the ability to connect with others on a profound level.

Set aside the tired notion that socialization can only occur within the confines of a classroom.

Unschoolers embrace the world as their classroom, where every encounter becomes an opportunity for growth and connection. Through real-life experiences and interactions, they learn to appreciate the vast diversity of the human experience and navigate the complexities of human relationships.

So, instead of questioning the socialization of Unschoolers, celebrate their unique path and recognize the wisdom in their unconventional approach. They are not isolated; they are deeply immersed in the fabric of society, forging meaningful connections and gaining invaluable life skills along the way. Embrace their journey and appreciate the depth and breadth of their socialization, as they flourish in the boundless realm of human connection.

Unschoolers Are Sheltered

How will Unschoolers with their sheltered background cope with the hardships of the real world? Let me debunk this common misconception that lingers in the minds of many. Unschoolers are not kept in isolation from the real world in a soft and cushioned environment as some people imagine. This notion, my dear reader, is nothing but a myth waiting to be shattered.

Unschoolers, unlike their schooled counterparts, are deeply immersed in the vibrant tapestry of the real world. They spend their entire time engaged in authentic experiences, exploring and learning from the world around them. While schooled kids may find themselves confined within the artificial microcosm of the school environment, surrounded only by peers of their own age and authority figures who rarely encourage questioning, Unschoolers embrace the full spectrum of human existence.

Living in the real world, Unschoolers encounter the challenges, complexities, and hardships that shape the human experience. They learn from firsthand interactions, observing and adapting to the ebb and flow of life's unpredictable circumstances. Instead of sheltering them from reality, Unschooling equips children with the resilience, adaptability, and problem-solving skills needed to navigate the complexities of the real world.

The truth is, Unschoolers emerge from their unconventional educational journey with a profound understanding of the real world. They have a diverse range of experiences, engaging with individuals of all ages, backgrounds, and walks of life. Their interactions teach them empathy, tolerance, and the ability to thrive amidst diversity.

So, let go of the notion that Unschoolers are ill-prepared for the hardships of the real world. They are 100% more equipped to face the challenges that come their way. Unschooling nurtures their curiosity, resourcefulness, and resilience, ensuring they are ready to embrace the ever-changing landscapes of life. It is within the unscripted journey of Unschooling that they forge their path, developing the skills and mindset needed to thrive in the real world's unpredictable terrain.

Fitting In When Out of School

Will Unschooling make my kids 'different' and unable to fit in with a crowd, work team, or social group? It's a question that lingers in the minds of many parents considering this educational path. But let me assure you, dear parents, that your kids are already part of a social group and a work team—the family. The family, as society's fundamental form of organization and connection, provides a solid foundation for social interaction and teamwork.

It's true that every work team and every 'gang' is unique, and just like anyone else, including those in traditional schooling, your children will need to adapt to different social groups. But here's the important point: Unschooling doesn't inhibit their ability to fit in—it empowers them to be true to themselves while navigating diverse social dynamics.

While conformity may be the norm for some, if your desire is for your children to simply follow the crowd and adjust themselves to fit any group they encounter, Unschooling may not align with your aspirations. Unschooling celebrates individuality and encourages self-expression, fostering a sense of authenticity and personal growth.

Through Unschooling, your children have the freedom to explore their passions, develop their unique talents, and forge their own identities. They learn to appreciate diversity, respect different perspectives, and find their place in a world that embraces individuality. These qualities will serve them well in any social setting, as they bring their authentic selves to the table.

Yes, Unschooling may make your kids 'different' in the eyes of some, but it's this very difference that cultivates resilience, empathy, and the ability to adapt to various social environments. They become confident individuals who can navigate the complexities of social interactions while staying true to their values and interests.

As you embark on the Unschooling journey with your children, embrace their uniqueness and celebrate their individuality. Unschooling equips them with the skills to forge meaningful connections, contribute to diverse teams, and thrive in social groups that value authenticity. Trust in their ability to navigate the world while staying true to themselves, and watch them blossom into confident, well-rounded individuals who leave a positive mark wherever they go.

The Question of School Safety

In certain areas, schools have gained a notorious reputation for being hotbeds of violence and danger. Tragically, incidents such as the Columbine massacre have cast a shadow over the perceived safety of traditional educational institutions. But do these public safety concerns drive parents to choose Unschooling as an alternative?

While it is true that schools in some neighborhoods may be deemed unsafe, it's important to note that, statistically speaking, schools still offer a relatively secure environment compared to the dangers of the streets. Instances of physical harm or violence occur less frequently within school walls than in the surrounding communities.

However, the decision to embrace Unschooling goes beyond solely prioritizing physical safety. Parents who choose Unschooling are motivated by a deeper desire for their children to experience a qualitatively different and enriching form of education. Unschooling recognizes that learning extends far beyond the confines of a traditional classroom. It acknowledges the importance of personalized, self-directed learning experiences that cater to each child's unique interests, passions, and learning styles.

Unschooling empowers parents to create a nurturing and supportive environment where their children can thrive intellectually, emotionally, and creatively. It encourages a love for learning, critical thinking skills, and the pursuit of knowledge that goes beyond rote memorization and standardized tests.

While concerns about public safety may play a role in some families' decision to pursue Unschooling, it is ultimately the desire to provide their children with a more holistic and individualized educational experience that drives them forward. Unschooling offers a transformative journey of intellectual exploration, personal growth, and the cultivation of a lifelong love for learning.

So, while the question of safety within schools may linger in the minds of some parents, it is the profound difference in the quality and nature of education that truly propels the Unschooling movement. It is a choice rooted in the belief that education should be a joyful and empowering journey, guided by the child's innate curiosity and thirst for knowledge.

In the realm of Unschooling, safety is just one piece of a larger puzzle—a puzzle that embraces the full potential of every child, nurtures their passions, and encourages them to become lifelong learners.

Dispelling the Myths

It is time to dispel a common misconception surrounding Unschoolers—that they are all Christian fundamentalists. Allow me to unravel this myth and reveal the vibrant tapestry of beliefs that exists within the Unschooling community.

While it is true that there are Christian Unschoolers, their presence is not indicative of a monolithic belief system. Unschoolers hail from a wide spectrum of Christian denominations, encompassing a rich diversity of perspectives and practices. To assume that all Unschoolers are Christian fundamentalists would be a disservice to the intricate mosaic of beliefs that intertwine within this educational philosophy.

In fact, the Unschooling community transcends religious affiliations. Unschoolers represent a tapestry of beliefs, spanning various spiritual traditions, as well as those who identify as entirely secular. Unschooling embraces families from all walks of life, from different cultural backgrounds, and with diverse religious and philosophical worldviews.

To paint Unschoolers with a broad brush of Christian fundamentalism is to overlook the vast expanse of beliefs and values that thrive within this educational approach. Unschooling is about individualized learning, tailored to the unique needs and interests of each child, irrespective of their religious or secular background.

Embrace the beautiful diversity that exists within the Unschooling community—a tapestry woven with myriad beliefs, perspectives, and cultural traditions. Unschooling celebrates the freedom to choose one's own path, be it shaped by faith, spirituality, or a wholly secular worldview. It is this diversity that enriches the tapestry of Unschooling and makes it a truly inclusive and empowering educational journey.

The Unschooling Dilemma

What do those who have walked the path of
Unschooling say is its most negative aspect?
It's a nuanced sentiment—a subtle twinge that
lingers, born from the realization that there
were certain courses or subjects that they were
not curious about during their unschooling
years. These topics remained undiscovered
until later in life, when they embarked on the
college journey and uncovered a genuine
affinity for them. In hindsight, they wish they
had engaged with these courses sooner.

Yet, let us ponder this observation. Is it truly a
shortcoming of Unschooling, or is it a
reminder that our own curiosity shapes our
learning journey? After all, it is not the
decision of an expert or the opinion of a

marketing guru that should dictate what captures our interest. Instead, it is the flame of curiosity within us that guides our path of discovery.

In the realm of Unschooling, we celebrate the individual's innate drive to explore and learn. It is a journey that embraces the pursuit of personal passions and the unraveling of one's unique intellectual tapestry. Unschoolers have the freedom to follow the threads of their curiosity, immersing themselves in subjects that truly resonate with their hearts and minds.

While it is true that there may be moments when hindsight reveals untapped interests, we must remember that our learning journey is a personal odyssey. It is shaped not by the prescribed agendas of others, but by our own organic quest for knowledge and understanding.

Let us celebrate the essence of Unschooling— a realm where curiosity is crowned king and personal exploration reigns supreme. Rather than dwelling on what might have been, let us bask in the exhilaration of our self-directed educational journeys. May we wholeheartedly embrace the freedom to discover, the power to choose, and the exquisite beauty of an education fueled by our innate curiosities. In these pursuits, we unlock the enchantment of true learning, forging an unbreakable bond between our souls and the boundless realms of knowledge that eagerly await our embrace.

Chapter 6 – The Legalities

Navigating the Legal Landscape

When it comes to the legal position of Unschoolers, it is essential to understand that Unschooling is classified as a form of homeschooling. Rest assured, Unschooling is legal in every state across the United States, as well as in numerous countries around the world.

For comprehensive information regarding homeschooling laws in different states, you can turn to the Home School Legal Defense Association (HSLDA) website. There, you will find detailed insights into the specific laws governing homeschooling in each state. Simply visit their website at https://www.hslda.org/laws/default.asp? to explore the legal landscape in your area.

It is worth noting that certain states impose specific requirements on homeschoolers, such as testing, reporting, or evaluation. The five most heavily regulated states in this regard are New York, Massachusetts, Pennsylvania, Vermont, and Rhode Island. Conversely, other states have more relaxed regulations, with minimal requirements for homeschooling or Unschooling.

Interestingly, eleven states even go a step further, not mandating homeschooling or Unschooling parents to notify state authorities about their educational approach. These states are Idaho, Alaska, Texas, Oklahoma, Missouri, Iowa, Illinois, Indiana, Michigan, Connecticut, and New Jersey.

However, it is crucial to keep in mind that laws can change regularly, and it is always wise to stay informed about the latest developments. While this information is accurate at the time of publication, I encourage you to reach out to your state representatives or local authorities to confirm the laws applicable in your specific state or country. Their expertise and guidance will ensure that you are well-versed in the legal requirements and can confidently pursue your Unschooling journey within the framework of the law.

Remember, knowledge is power, and understanding the legal landscape empowers Unschoolers to navigate the educational journey with confidence and peace of mind.

School Authorities

The opinions of school authorities and education bureaucrats regarding Unschooling are quite diverse. While there are those who harbor hostility towards this alternative approach to education, and others who remain indifferent, it is important to note that many individuals in positions of power within the education system have developed a deep respect for Unschooling parents and their right to choose this path for their children.

This respect stems from the recognition that the Unschooling movement injects a vibrant energy into the ongoing debate surrounding the realities and tensions within the realm of traditional schooling. By challenging conventional notions of education, Unschooling prompts important discussions and reflections on the effectiveness of our current systems.

It is within this backdrop of differing perspectives that Unschooling continues to carve its path, fostering an environment where parents can confidently embark on their own unique educational journey with their children.

The Role of Teaching Credentials

Delving into the realm of Unschooling raises a thought-provoking question: Should Unschooling situations require credentialed teachers? Is it necessary for the teacher-parent to possess official teaching credentials in order to facilitate their children's Unschooling journey?

The answer lies within a complex landscape, as the efficacy of traditional schooling and teaching credentials itself has been subject to scrutiny. It's undeniable that not all credentialed teachers in public schools consistently deliver a high-quality education. This realization prompts parents to explore alternative paths, such as Unschooling, seeking an educational approach that resonates with their values and aspirations.

Unschooling parents contend that obtaining teaching credentials wouldn't necessarily enhance their ability to navigate their children's Unschooling experience. They question whether these credentials truly contribute to effective time management or the creation of intricate lesson plans. Instead, they emphasize their dedication, commitment, and their own well-rounded education as crucial factors in providing their children with a rich and meaningful educational journey.

Furthermore, Unschooling parents advocate for a broader perspective on education. They propose a shift in focus towards improving teaching quality within traditional school systems, rather than imposing unnecessary restrictions on dedicated parents who have chosen the path of Unschooling. By directing efforts towards enhancing educational standards and fostering an environment of continuous improvement, both traditional schools and Unschooling can benefit.

Unschooling invites us to challenge conventional norms and explore innovative approaches that align with the unique needs of each child. It emphasizes a personalized approach to learning, where education extends beyond formal certifications. Unschooling recognizes that the true essence of education lies in nurturing curiosity, fostering a love for learning, and embracing diverse educational experiences.

In this ongoing conversation, it is crucial to engage in open-minded dialogue and cultivate an environment where various perspectives can be shared. By embracing a holistic view of education and valuing the commitment and passion of parents, we can collectively strive towards creating an educational landscape that empowers children to embark on their own unique paths, whether within the boundaries of traditional schooling or the uncharted territories of Unschooling.

Unschooling and Legal Outcomes

In the realm of Unschooling, it is important to acknowledge that challenges and legal disputes may arise. These cases, though not representative of the broader Unschooling movement, shed light on the complexities surrounding homeschooling and the concerns raised by authorities.

One such case, originating from California, serves as an example of the adversities faced by Unschooling families. California, often regarded as a hub of progressive developments, has an estimated 17,000 children being educated at home by their parents, with numbers steadily rising.

In 2010, the California Court of Appeal made a ruling that homeschooling parents do not possess constitutional rights to educate their children without a teaching credential. This ruling emerged from a child welfare dispute involving the County Department of Children and Family Services in Los Angeles and a couple who were practicing Unschooling with their eight children.

The investigation stemmed from allegations of physical and emotional abuse by the father. As a result, the Department of Social Services intervened, leading the case to be brought before a judge for dependency hearings. During these proceedings, the court examined the relationship between the parents and their children, and one significant finding pertained to the Unschooling approach implemented by the mother. Consequently, all eight children were either enrolled in a public school or provided tutoring by individuals with teaching credentials.

The judge's ruling deemed the education the children were receiving to be inadequate, criticizing its quality and substance. While recognizing that parents have a constitutional right to homeschool their children, the judge highlighted the state's prerogative to ensure a minimum standard of education. This balancing act between parental rights and the state's responsibility to safeguard educational standards has been addressed in previous rulings, including the landmark case of Pierce v. The Society of Sisters in the 1920s, which affirmed a citizen's right to make choices regarding their children's education while allowing the state to regulate educational quality.

It is crucial to note that these legal requirements do not inherently contradict the constitutional rights of parents in determining their children's education. Rather, they serve as a mechanism to ensure that children receive a basic level of education as mandated by the state.

Similar rulings have emerged in the past, underscoring the ongoing dialogue and tension surrounding the rights of parents, the role of the state, and the pursuit of quality education.

While it is essential to recognize these legal outcomes, it is equally important to approach them with a nuanced perspective. They represent individual cases within a broader landscape, and they should not overshadow the vast array of successful Unschooling experiences that empower children to thrive in unconventional educational environments.

As the Unschooling movement evolves, it is crucial to foster open dialogue and engage in constructive conversations that promote understanding and advocate for the rights of parents while ensuring the best interests and educational welfare of the children. Through a balanced and informed approach, we can navigate the challenges that arise and continue striving for educational freedom and innovation.

The Amish's Landmark Case

The roots of Unschooling can be traced back to a particular group of people who were among its early proponents—the Amish community. Their pivotal role in shaping the concept of Unschooling can be seen through a landmark court case that captured the nation's attention in 1972: "Wisconsin vs. Yoder."

At the heart of this case were three Amish parents who had chosen to Unschool their children, refusing to send them to school beyond the eighth grade. Rooted in their deeply held religious beliefs, the Amish parents believed that the education imparted within the confines of their own homes far surpassed the worldly knowledge taught in traditional schools.

However, their decision to withdraw their children from school led to their conviction in a Wisconsin county court, resulting in a nominal fine of five dollars each. Undeterred, they took their case to the Wisconsin Supreme Court, seeking justice and the recognition of their rights as parents to homeschool, including the practice of Unschooling.

In a groundbreaking ruling, the Wisconsin Supreme Court overturned the previous verdict, acknowledging the Amish parents' claim that the application of compulsory school attendance laws infringed upon their rights. Citing the Free Exercise Clause of the First Amendment to the US Constitution, which had been made applicable to the States through the Fourteenth Amendment, the court affirmed the parents' right to educate their children in accordance with their religious beliefs.

The significance of this case extended far beyond the boundaries of Wisconsin. The State, dissatisfied with the ruling, appealed to the highest judicial authority in the land—the US Supreme Court.

The Amish parents' fight for the right to Unschool their children had captured the attention of the entire nation. The outcome of this case would not only shape the trajectory of Unschooling but also set a precedent for the rights of parents to choose alternative forms of education for their children.

In the next chapter of the Unschooling journey, the US Supreme Court would have the final say, determining the fate of the Amish parents' quest for educational freedom and paving the way for the broader recognition of Unschooling as a legitimate and constitutionally protected form of education.

Victory for Educational Freedom

With the eyes of the nation fixed upon them, the moment of truth had arrived. The fate of the Amish parents and their right to Unschool their children hung in the balance. All hopes were pinned on the eminent justices of the US Supreme Court as they deliberated over the case of "Wisconsin vs. Yoder."

And then, like a resounding echo of justice, the decision was rendered. In a unanimous ruling, the highest court in the land affirmed the judgment of the Wisconsin Supreme Court, delivering a historic victory for the defendants—Jonas Yoder, Wallace Miller, and Adin Yutzy.

The US Supreme Court upheld the fundamental rights of these brave parents, recognizing and honoring their deeply held religious beliefs. The verdict echoed through the hallowed halls of justice, reverberating with the resounding proclamation that parents possess the inherent authority to educate their children outside the confines of traditional schooling.

The Amish parents, who had stood their ground against the coercive forces of the state, emerged triumphant. Their five-dollar fines were rightfully returned to them, symbolizing not just a nominal restitution but a symbolic restoration of their dignity and autonomy as parents.

More significantly, this landmark ruling solidified the recognition of Unschooling as a legitimate educational choice, safeguarded by the constitutional principles of religious freedom and parental rights. The decision marked a turning point in the educational landscape, affirming the notion that education extends far beyond the walls of a traditional classroom.

With this resounding victory, the path was cleared for countless other families to exercise their right to Unschool their children. The spirit of educational freedom soared, and the voices of parents advocating for alternative forms of education grew louder and stronger.

In the tapestry of American history, the case of "Wisconsin vs. Yoder" became a vibrant thread, interwoven with the values of liberty, diversity, and the pursuit of individualized education. It was a testament to the enduring spirit of a nation founded on the principles of freedom, a reminder that the collective voice of the people can shape the course of justice.

As the gavel struck the final chord, the Amish parents and their fellow Unschoolers rejoiced, their faith in the power of the people and the resilience of the American legal system reaffirmed. In this momentous triumph, the heart of America beat a little stronger, as the torch of educational freedom illuminated the path for future generations.

God bless America, indeed, for within its borders, the seeds of liberty continue to flourish, nurturing the growth of an educational landscape that celebrates individuality, choice, and the unyielding spirit of those who dare to question, to challenge, and to Unschool.

Addressing Child Abuse

Child abuse is a grave concern that demands our attention, regardless of the educational setting. It is essential to address this issue and ensure the safety and well-being of all children, including those in Unschooling environments.

In the United States, there are between one and two million children who are either Unschooled or homeschooled. While it is true that cases of child abuse may occur within these settings, it is important to avoid sensationalism and not draw hasty conclusions about the prevalence of abuse in Unschooling households compared to traditional schooling environments.

To claim that Unschooling children are at a higher risk of abuse than their Schooled counterparts lacks empirical evidence. Child abuse is a societal issue that transcends educational choices. Sadly, instances of abuse can occur in any setting, including public schools.

It is crucial to recognize that child abuse can often go unnoticed or unreported, irrespective of the educational context. Public schools do not guarantee the prevention of child abuse, nor can we attribute a lower incidence of abuse solely to the schooling system.

Addressing child abuse requires a comprehensive and multifaceted approach that involves proactive measures, community awareness, and a collective commitment to protecting the well-being of children. This responsibility falls upon society as a whole, not solely on specific educational models.

In the Unschooling community, as in any other, the emphasis should be on creating a safe and nurturing environment for children. It is incumbent upon parents, caregivers, and the broader community to be vigilant, to promote open communication, and to report any suspected cases of child abuse to the appropriate authorities.

By fostering a culture of safety, awareness, and support, we can work together to protect the rights and well-being of all children, regardless of their chosen educational path. Let us continue to prioritize the safety and welfare of our children, ensuring that they grow up in environments where their voices are heard, their well-being is protected, and their potential is nurtured.

The Freedom to Educate My Child

What if there are parents who resist allowing their children to conform to the standard education dictated by the state? That question strikes at the heart of the matter.

Unschoolers passionately assert that the state, regardless of its constitutional authority, has no right to intrude upon or dictate the content and methods of their children's education. According to John Gatto's compelling arguments, centralized state interference in education is the culmination of a century-long conspiracy orchestrated by influential industrialists and their political and academic accomplices. Their aim? To forge a society comprised of docile individuals devoid of critical thinking, reduced to mere consumers rather than independent producers.

In the words of Ivan Illich, a prominent Deschooler, it is time to challenge the state's presumed authority over education. He advocates for the constitutional disestablishment of the school's monopoly, dismantling a system that intertwines prejudice with discrimination. In envisioning a modern, humanist society, Illich proposes a fundamental principle akin to the First Amendment of the U.S. Constitution: "The State shall make no law with respect to the establishment of education." A society that truly values individual liberty must reject the imposition of mandatory rituals that stifle personal growth and expression.

Unschooling stands as a defiant affirmation of the right to nurture and guide our children's educational journey free from state interference. It embodies the belief that parents, as the primary advocates for their children's well-being, possess the wisdom and responsibility to provide an education that aligns with their values, aspirations, and unique needs.

The battle for educational freedom rages on, challenging the status quo and questioning the assumed authority of the state. It is a battle fueled by the conviction that education should not be a one-size-fits-all system, but rather a diverse tapestry woven by the individual choices and aspirations of each child. Let us rally together in defense of our right to shape the educational landscape, rejecting the notion of a compulsory, uniform education dictated by external forces. For in doing so, we cultivate a society that cherishes the pursuit of knowledge, celebrates individuality, and upholds the values of freedom and self-determination.

Chapter 7 – Parent Teacher

Embracing the Role of Teacher

In the realm of Unschooling, the question arises: Will there still be teachers? In this imaginative landscape, the answer takes a fascinating turn. In a world where Unschooling prevails, everyone becomes a teacher.

I firmly believe that each and every one of us possesses a unique expertise or skill. To teach is to share the knowledge we have acquired through our personal journeys. In this Unschooling utopia, the act of teaching becomes a collective endeavor, a tapestry woven by the diverse talents and passions of individuals.

Gone are the traditional boundaries that confined teaching to a select few who held formal credentials. Instead, the role of a teacher transcends the confines of a classroom. It becomes an integral part of our everyday lives, an opportunity to ignite curiosity and inspire others with the wisdom we have gained.

In this world, teaching becomes a reciprocal exchange, an ongoing dialogue that enriches both the teacher and the learner. It is no longer limited to a structured educational setting but emerges organically from the fabric of our interactions and shared experiences.

Imagine a society where parents teach their children, neighbors impart their specialized knowledge, and mentors guide the eager minds of the younger generation. Each interaction becomes an opportunity for growth, a chance to expand our horizons and deepen our understanding of the world.

In this Unschooling world, the traditional concept of a teacher transforms into something more profound—a catalyst for intellectual growth, a source of inspiration, and a facilitator of lifelong learning.

While this vision remains speculative, it ignites our imagination and reminds us of the profound capacity we all possess to teach and learn from one another. It prompts us to recognize the inherent value of our unique perspectives and encourages us to embrace the role of a teacher in shaping a brighter future for generations to come.

Journey of Shared Learning

Embarking on the Unschooling journey without prior teaching experience can seem like a daunting prospect. It's natural to wonder how you can guide your child's learning when you may not possess expertise in all areas of knowledge. However, it's important to remember that even in traditional school settings, teachers don't possess all-encompassing knowledge either. No one does.

When your curious little Unschooler poses questions about topics you may not be familiar with, embrace the opportunity to embark on a learning adventure together. Unschooling thrives on the principle of honesty and genuine exploration. Instead of providing a superficial answer or feigning expertise, you can openly acknowledge that you don't know the answer right away. This paves the way for a collaborative learning experience where you and your child can embark on a quest to discover the answers together.

By engaging in this process, you demonstrate the value of curiosity, critical thinking, and the joy of lifelong learning. You set an example of intellectual humility and the willingness to explore new territories of knowledge. Your child will witness firsthand that it's okay not to have all the answers and that learning is an ongoing journey filled with exciting discoveries.

In the realm of Unschooling, the focus shifts from the teacher being the sole source of knowledge to fostering an environment where learning becomes a shared exploration. You become a guide, facilitator, and co-learner, fostering a deep connection and mutual growth between you and your child.

So, rest assured that not having all the answers shouldn't discourage you from embracing Unschooling. It's an opportunity to embark on a remarkable educational adventure, where both you and your child can thrive, learn, and discover together. Embrace the unknown, celebrate curiosity, and let the wonders of Unschooling unfold before your eyes.

Full-Time Parent-Teacher

Stepping into the role of a full-time Unschooling parent-teacher is an exhilarating voyage, filled with moments of confidence and moments of uncertainty. It is a path where we, as parents, embrace the profound responsibility of shaping our children's education, equipping them with the tools they need for any path they choose in life.

For some of us, confidence emanates from the deep conviction that we are charting the right course for our children. We recognize that by embracing Unschooling, we are providing them with a holistic education—one that nurtures their unique talents, passions, and potential. We understand that traditional career paths may lie ahead, or perhaps our children will embark on a more unconventional and unpredictable journey. Regardless, we are confident that the foundation we lay will empower them to thrive in any endeavor they undertake.

Yet, for others, the transition into full-time Unschooling can be a formidable challenge. We grapple with ingrained assumptions that education must be entrusted to strangers adorned with the trappings of authority and expertise. We wrestle with self-doubt, questioning whether we possess the knowledge and skills to guide our children's learning. But gradually, with each passing day spent engaging in our children's educational journey, that lack of confidence begins to dissipate.

As we immerse ourselves in the daily rhythm of learning alongside our children, we discover the immense power that lies within us. We witness firsthand the growth and progress they make under our loving guidance. We realize that our deep connection with our children, fueled by unwavering dedication and genuine care, is the foundation upon which their education thrives.

Unschooling is not a solitary endeavor but a shared experience, an ongoing dialogue between parent and child. It is a journey of mutual discovery, where we learn alongside our children, drawing inspiration from their curiosity and expanding our own horizons in the process.

As full-time Unschooling parent-teachers, we learn to embrace the challenges and celebrate the triumphs. We navigate uncharted territories, breaking free from societal norms and forging a unique path for our children. With each passing day, our confidence grows, and we witness the profound impact of our unwavering commitment to our children's educational journey.

Parent-Teacher of an Unschooler

What does it take to step into the role of a parent-teacher for an Unschooler? Let me assure you that it does not require great wealth, an esteemed education, or a lofty social position. No, the foundation of this remarkable journey lies in one's unwavering devotion to their children.

To embark on this path, you need not break the world down into sterile worksheets and standardized tests. Instead, you delve into the depths of your child's passions, immersing yourself completely in their unique interests. It is as if you are handing them the entire world, allowing them to explore its wonders and connect their passions to every facet of life.

Unschooler parent-teachers firmly believe that this approach nurtures their children into independent, self-supporting individuals who never lose their love for learning. Our culture has ingrained in us the notion that institutions and systems hold the key to our children's education. We are led to believe that there are professionals better equipped to teach our children than we are. But as Unschooler parent-teachers, we have broken free from this narrative.

We place our trust in our children and the inherent wisdom within them. We recognize that they possess an innate desire to learn and grow. Our role is to provide them with the resources they need, to be attentive to their requests and curiosities, and to facilitate their exploration of the world around them. We become their guides, their advocates, and their partners in the journey of self-discovery.

To be a parent-teacher of an Unschooler is to embrace a profound trust in the capabilities and potential of your child. It is to let go of preconceived notions and embrace the limitless possibilities that unfold when a child is given the freedom to pursue their passions. It is a journey that requires open-mindedness, adaptability, and a willingness to break free from the confines of traditional educational paradigms.

So if you aspire to become a parent-teacher of an Unschooler, prepare to embark on a path of devotion and trust. Embrace the boundless curiosity and unwavering spirit of your child. Provide them with the resources they seek, support their exploration, and watch as they blossom into independent learners, driven by their innate love for knowledge. Together, you will forge a remarkable educational journey— one that celebrates the unique potential of every child and ignites a lifelong passion for learning.

Unschooling When We Work

The question arises: Can I embark on the Unschooling journey if my partner and I both have to work? Or what if I am single-handedly navigating the realms of work and raising my child?

The resounding answer is: Yes, you can. Many individuals have successfully walked this path, navigating the intricacies of balancing work commitments and the profound responsibility of guiding their child's education. It may require a delicate dance of time management and innovative solutions, but rest assured, it is indeed possible.

One avenue to explore is the realm of flexible work arrangements. Seek opportunities that allow for part-time or freelance work, granting you the freedom to actively participate in your child's educational journey. Embrace the challenge of finding creative ways to earn a living while ensuring quality time for learning and exploration.

Additionally, consider the power of community and collaboration. Connect with like-minded individuals who share similar circumstances and form a co-op. Through this cooperative effort, working parents can come together, exchanging homes and support to ensure that someone is always present for the children. This community-driven approach not only enriches the learning experience but also cultivates a sense of belonging and support.

In cases where your child is of an age and maturity level to stay home alone, this can be an option worth considering. However, it is essential to familiarize yourself with your state's laws and regulations regarding the appropriate age and guidelines for unsupervised periods.

Remember, the Unschooling journey is a testament to the resilience and resourcefulness of both parent and child. It is a testament to our unwavering commitment to nurturing a love for learning in the midst of life's demands. So, fear not, for you can embark on this transformative path, weaving together the tapestry of work and Unschooling, and embracing the boundless possibilities that await both you and your child.

Unschooling During Life's Demands

In Unschooling, the notion of subjects becomes fluid and expansive. Rather than confining learning within the boundaries of traditional subject areas, Unschooling encourages a broader perspective, one that encompasses the interconnectedness of knowledge and the rich tapestry of human experience.

Subjects are artificial constructs created by educational systems to compartmentalize knowledge. Unschooling challenges this approach by recognizing that real-life learning transcends the boundaries of subjects. Instead, it honors the innate curiosity of the child and encourages exploration across a wide range of interests, allowing for a multidisciplinary approach that weaves together different fields of knowledge.

By embracing this holistic approach, Unschoolers embark on a profound educational journey that encourages them to delve into their passions and follow the threads of curiosity wherever they may lead. Whether it's science, art, history, or technology, Unschooling allows children to engage with their interests in a deep and meaningful way, fostering a love of learning that extends far beyond the confines of traditional subjects.

Furthermore, Unschooling recognizes that knowledge is interconnected. A child's exploration of a particular interest naturally leads to the discovery of related concepts and disciplines. This integrated approach to learning fosters a deeper understanding of the interconnectedness of the world, nurturing critical thinking skills and encouraging a holistic view of knowledge.

In Unschooling, education is not confined to the boundaries of subjects. Instead, it becomes a vibrant and dynamic exploration of the world, where the child's interests and passions serve as the compass for their learning journey. By embracing this multifaceted tapestry of knowledge, Unschoolers unlock the true potential of education, fostering a lifelong love for learning and a deep appreciation for the interconnectedness of all subjects and disciplines.

It's time to release the constraints of traditional subjects and embrace the multifaceted nature of Unschooling. Celebrate the interconnectedness of knowledge and empower your children to explore the vast tapestry of human understanding. In doing so, we unlock the true potential of education, nurturing curious minds and fostering a love for learning that knows no boundaries.

Navigating the Boundaries

Ah, the delicate dance of setting boundaries in the realm of Unschooling—a realm where freedom and self-directed learning intertwine. As an Unschooling parent-teacher, I am entrusted with the task of fostering a nurturing learning environment while respecting the innate curiosity and autonomy of my child. But how do we navigate this uncharted territory?

In the vast spectrum of Unschooling, there exists a range of approaches to boundary-setting. Some may opt for a mildly strict stance, while others embrace a philosophy of total liberation. The key lies in finding the right balance, for the learning community that blossoms within an Unschooler family thrives on harmony and mutual respect.

While children are naturally wired to learn and explore, there are moments when gentle guidance can help maintain equilibrium. As a parent-teacher, I may find it beneficial to establish certain limitations that promote environmental awareness and physical development. For instance, I might set boundaries around the use of television, or the amount of time devoted to technology, understanding that balance is crucial for a well-rounded learning experience.

However, it is essential to recognize that there is no one-size-fits-all formula when it comes to boundary-setting in Unschooling. The beauty of this approach lies in its flexibility, allowing each family to craft their own unique path. What works for one child may not resonate with another, and that is perfectly acceptable.

In the realm of Unschooling, boundaries are not rigid walls confining the learner but rather gentle signposts that guide their journey. They serve as reminders, nudging us to strike a harmonious balance between freedom and responsibility. They are not imposed from above but emerge organically from the needs and dynamics of our learning community.

As an Unschooling parent-teacher, I cherish the opportunity to co-create an environment where my child can thrive intellectually, emotionally, and creatively. I understand that boundaries are not meant to restrict or stifle their innate curiosity but to provide a supportive structure within which they can explore and grow.

Through open communication, mutual understanding, and a deep respect for each other's perspectives, we find our way in this uncharted territory of Unschooling. We engage in ongoing dialogue, adjusting boundaries as we learn and evolve together. It is a dynamic process, an ever-shifting dance that embraces the ebb and flow of our shared journey.

When you embark on this remarkable adventure, remember you hold the delicate balance between freedom and guidance. Let us celebrate the freedom to learn, explore, and discover, while gently guiding our children towards a holistic educational experience. In this realm of Unschooling, boundaries become beacons of balance, nurturing the growth of our young learners, and fostering a lifelong love for knowledge.

Never Too Late to Start

In the realm of Unschooling, the notion of age as a limiting factor simply melts away. It embraces the belief that learning knows no boundaries of time or age, and thus, it is never too late to embark on the path of Unschooling.

Even if one has endured the conventional schooling experience, labeled as "old-school," the transformative power of Unschooling can still weave its magic. Unschooling recognizes that the scars inflicted by the competitive and coercive nature of traditional education can be addressed and healed. It acknowledges the potential psychological wounds caused by the relentless testing, grading, evaluation, and the subsequent erosion of self-esteem and confidence.

Unschooling becomes a beacon of hope, illuminating the path towards reclaiming one's innate love for learning, irrespective of past experiences. It encourages individuals to shed the shackles of rigid curriculum and embrace a personalized and self-directed journey of exploration and growth.

In the realm of Unschooling, knowledge is not confined to textbooks or limited to the confines of a classroom. It flourishes through real-world experiences, personal interests, and the pursuit of genuine passions. Unschooling invites individuals to cultivate their curiosity, embrace autonomy, and nurture a lifelong love for learning.

So, whether you have traversed the corridors of the traditional schooling system or find yourself yearning for a different approach to education, Unschooling extends its open arms, welcoming you into a world of limitless possibilities. It embarks on a journey of healing, rekindling the flame of learning, and empowering individuals to reclaim their intellectual autonomy. For in the realm of Unschooling, it is never too late to embrace the transformative power of education and embark on a path of self-discovery and growth.

Chapter 8– But I'm Not a Teacher

Unschooling and Math

One of the greatest challenges lies in teaching a wide array of subjects. Among them, mathematics takes center stage, sparking debates and raising questions. Can a child truly grasp the intricacies of math without formal instruction? Let us delve into this captivating topic and unravel the possibilities that Unschooling holds.

Learning is driven by curiosity and the innate quest for understanding. Children naturally gravitate towards subjects that ignite their interest and align with their aspirations. When it comes to mathematics, the key lies in providing experiences that pave the way for mathematical discovery.

It is true that not everyone is born a mathematician, just as not everyone is born an artist. Each child possesses unique strengths and inclinations—some lean towards analytical thinking, while others embrace their creative spirit. Unschooling celebrates this diversity, granting children the freedom to explore their own aptitudes and interests.

Through self-directed learning, Unschoolers have the opportunity to unlock their mathematical potential. When faced with challenges or goals that require advanced mathematical knowledge, their intrinsic motivation propels them to seek the necessary skills. Just as they would tackle any other subject, they embark on a journey of discovery, driven by their own aspirations.

In the Unschooling approach, math becomes a tool that children wield to further their understanding of the world. It is not imposed upon them but emerges as a natural consequence of their inquisitive exploration. As they engage in real-life situations, apply mathematical principles, and solve problems that resonate with their own experiences, their mathematical proficiency blossoms.

Try to embrace the idea that mathematics can indeed be learned informally. By fostering an environment that nurtures curiosity and encourages exploration, we empower our Unschoolers to discover their own unique path to mathematical understanding. Together, we unlock the doors to a world where mathematics becomes not just a subject, but a powerful tool for comprehending and shaping the world around us.

Making Math Come Alive

Let's venture into the world of Unschooler Math, where numbers come alive and learning becomes an exhilarating adventure. In this mindset, we embrace a different approach, one that sparks curiosity and engages young minds in the wonders of mathematics. No, this is not a fairytale, but a real and captivating journey.

Unschooling invites us to go beyond symbols and formulas and embrace the power of play and hands-on experiences. We understand that true understanding flourishes when children can explore and interact with math in meaningful ways. So, we weave math into their everyday adventures, where equations dance with imagination and numbers become their trusted companions.

Picture a child stepping into the realm of addition and subtraction, not through lifeless equations, but through vibrant storytelling. Here, knights battle dragons, each encounter an opportunity to unlock the mysteries of arithmetic. As our young learners immerse themselves in these imaginative tales, they effortlessly grasp the essence of mathematical operations and witness the magic of numbers.

Unschooler Math is a celebration of creative exploration. We tap into children's boundless curiosity and natural instincts, nurturing their understanding of math through real-world experiences. From counting seashells on the shore to measuring ingredients in the kitchen, every moment becomes an invitation to discover the beauty of mathematics in their daily lives.

This approach kindles a love affair between young minds and the enchanting world of numbers. It transcends the confines of textbooks and sterile classrooms, offering a transformative journey where math intertwines with the fabric of their existence. As parents and guides, we unlock the doors to mathematical wonders, igniting a passion that extends beyond the boundaries of traditional education.

In this extraordinary odyssey, our Unschoolers embark on a quest of self-discovery. We celebrate the diversity of their minds, acknowledging that not everyone is born a mathematician, just as not everyone is born an artist. Unschooling grants them the freedom to explore their interests, forge their own paths, and embrace their unique mathematical identity.

Allow math to take you on an adventure. Set sail on this voyage of numerical wonders. Illuminate the world with the brilliance of mathematical exploration for your child, nurturing a lifelong love for the beauty and intrigue that numbers hold. With each playful moment, we empower our young learners to unlock the boundless potential that lies within the captivating realm of Unschooler Math.

Living In Numbers Daily

Is it possible for children to learn math on their own? Many believe that math is a challenging subject to grasp, as it seems disconnected from our daily experiences. However, I assure you, this notion couldn't be further from the truth.

You see, numbers and their intricate relationships surround children in their everyday lives, painting a vivid picture of the world's boundaries and possibilities. From the patterns in nature to the rhythms of music, mathematics intertwines with the fabric of their existence, making it a visible and tangible force.

Moreover, number references seamlessly weave themselves into the very language children are in the process of mastering. As they learn to communicate and express themselves, numerical concepts become an intrinsic part of their linguistic exploration. It is through this organic integration of numbers and language that children effortlessly relate to the mathematical realm.

In fact, it is worth noting that children inherently possess a natural affinity for numbers. They possess an intuitive understanding of quantity and can effortlessly navigate basic mathematical concepts. It is only when these concepts are stripped of their familiarity and presented in the form of sterile school worksheets and intimidating test questions that they appear foreign and distant.

Therefore, rest assured that children have an innate ability to relate to numbers and engage with the world of mathematics. It is our duty as educators to nurture this natural connection and create an environment where math is approached with curiosity and excitement. By embracing real-life applications, incorporating playful activities, and fostering a sense of relevance, we can empower children to discover the beauty and significance of math on their own terms.

So let us debunk the myth that math is an impenetrable fortress. Instead, let us celebrate the inherent mathematical curiosity within every child and embark on a journey of exploration and discovery together. Through nurturing their innate mathematical abilities and dismantling the barriers of formal instruction, we can unlock a world of numerical wonders, empowering children to embrace math with confidence and joy.

Journey of Reading and Writing

A burning question often arises: How do children learn to read and write? Is it something they must be explicitly taught, or can they simply pick it up on their own? In the enchanting world of learning, renowned educators Gatto and Holt passionately advocate for the natural acquisition of reading skills, even from texts that some experts deem too advanced for young minds. Join me as we unravel the mysteries of this captivating topic and explore the fascinating journey of literacy.

When children are immersed in a world of written words, something magical happens. Driven by their innate curiosity, they embark on a quest to decipher the meanings behind those mysterious symbols. Through observation, imitation, and the gentle support of adults, they gradually unravel the secrets of reading and writing. It is not traditional teaching in the strict sense, but rather a nurturing environment that allows their natural instincts to flourish. Together, we shall discover the profound connection between curiosity and literacy.

In Waldorf Education, a unique approach to reading emerges. Here, the art of reading is not introduced until the age of seven, coinciding with a significant milestone known as the "change of teeth." This deliberate timing allows children to fully develop their capacities and explore the world through other senses before delving into the written word. We shall delve into the wisdom behind this approach and unravel the remarkable outcomes it produces.

Contrary to popular belief, there is substantial evidence that children who learn to read relatively late are not at a disadvantage. In fact, they have the remarkable ability to quickly catch up and even surpass their peers who started reading earlier. These late bloomers often avoid the fatigue and disinterest that can plague those who were pushed into reading prematurely. Their passion for reading and learning remains vibrant throughout their lives, painting a vivid picture of the long-term benefits of following one's natural rhythm.

When reading is not forced or imposed, a healthy child naturally and effortlessly picks it up. Through this organic process, children develop a profound connection with books, devouring their pages with voracious enthusiasm. Though some Waldorf parents may initially feel anxious if their child takes longer to learn to read, they are eventually overcome with joy when witnessing their little ones immerse themselves in the written word. Each child has their own optimal time to "take off" on their literary voyage, and it is essential for parents to navigate their own concerns and support their child's unique journey.

In the intricate tapestry of human growth and development, linear progression and measurable benchmarks do not hold sway. Instead, we must grasp the ineffable nature of human life and its inherent metamorphic laws. In this final chapter, we explore the profound depths of human potential and the immeasurable beauty that resides within each individual. Let us revel in the mystery and wonder of the human experience as we unlock the true essence of literacy.

As we conclude our exploration of natural literacy, we are left with a deep appreciation for the innate capacities of young minds. By nurturing their curiosity, honoring their unique timing, and creating an environment rich in written words, we unlock the door to a world of limitless possibilities. Let us celebrate the power of natural learning and embark on a lifelong journey of literacy, guided by the invisible yet transformative forces that shape our human existence.

The Unique Rhythm of Reading

As an Unschooling parent, you may find
yourself pondering a common question: What
if my child still can't read at the age of nine?
Fear not, for the journey of literacy unfolds at
its own exquisite pace, guided by the unique
rhythm of your child's development.

In Unschooling, we relinquish the confines of
fixed age expectations and embrace the
fluidity of learning. The art of reading, like
any other skill, blooms within each child's
heart when the time is right. It is a delicate
melody that echoes through the chambers of
their mind, waiting to be sung.

There is no predetermined age by which a
child must master the art of reading. Instead,
we honor their individual journey and allow

them to chart their own course through the realms of literacy. Let go of societal pressures and predetermined timelines, for they hold no sway in the expansive landscape of Unschooling.

Observe your child with gentle curiosity, attuning yourself to the signs and signals that reveal their readiness for reading. Every child possesses a unique tapestry of strengths and challenges, and their journey towards literacy will unfold in its own wondrous way.

As an Unschooling parent, your role is not to impose or force the acquisition of reading skills, but to create a rich and nurturing environment that inspires a love for words. Surround your child with books, engage in captivating stories, and foster a love for language. Allow their curiosity to lead the way, for it is through their natural inclination to explore that the seeds of literacy will take root.

Should your child's journey towards reading extend beyond what may be considered "typical" timelines, trust in their innate ability to find their way. Each child possesses an internal compass that guides them towards their unique milestones. By relinquishing control and embracing their individual rhythm, you grant them the freedom to flourish in their own time.

Remember that the joy of reading lies not in the age at which it is acquired, but in the boundless worlds it unveils. It is a lifelong journey, an ever-unfolding tapestry of exploration and understanding. Trust in the process, for when the time is right, your child will embark on their literary voyage with unwavering enthusiasm.

If doubts or concerns linger, seek solace in the wisdom of others who have treaded this path before. Explore the rich resources available, such as the article found at the following link:

http://blog.bellalunatoys.com/2011/waldorf-reading.html

Within its pages, you may discover insights and perspectives that illuminate your path and offer reassurance in nurturing literacy through Unschooling.

Don't get caught up worrying about the pace at which your child embraces the art of reading.

Embrace the fluidity of their learning journey, celebrating the unique rhythm that guides them. With patience, love, and an unwavering belief in their innate potential, you will witness the blossoming of a lifelong love affair with the written word.

Subject Choices

A question that often arises is whether it's possible to embrace the Unschooling philosophy for some areas, such as biology, while adhering to a more traditional curriculum for subjects like math. The answer, my curious companions, is yes, it's indeed feasible. However, we must tread carefully, for we risk allowing the rigid structure of formal schooling to seep into the vibrant tapestry of child-led learning that Unschooling embodies.

Unschooling, at its core, celebrates the spirit of freedom and self-directed exploration. It encourages a partnership between parent and child, fostering an environment where learning becomes a joyful journey guided by the child's passions and curiosities. When we introduce a fixed and top-down curriculum, we risk diluting the essence of Unschooling and impeding the organic flow of discovery.

In biology, for instance, we can embrace Unschooling's principles by immersing ourselves in the wonders of the natural world. We venture into nature, observe the intricate ecosystems, and engage in hands-on experiences that nurture our understanding of life's mysteries. Through field trips, experiments, and discussions, we awaken a profound connection with the biological realm, fostering a deep appreciation for the wonders of existence.

Now, let us turn our gaze to mathematics, a subject often associated with a more structured approach. While it may seem tempting to introduce a formal curriculum, we must pause and reflect on the spirit of Unschooling. It calls upon us to view math through a different lens, to uncover its inherent beauty and practical applications through everyday experiences.

In the Unschooling realm, math becomes intertwined with our daily lives. We explore geometric shapes in architecture, we calculate measurements in the kitchen, and we embrace the patterns found in nature. By integrating math seamlessly into our activities, we honor the child's natural inclination to understand the world through numbers and equations.

However, we must approach this dance of subject choices with mindful intention. We must ensure that our partnership with our child remains rooted in the principles of Unschooling. The freedom to explore, the joy of self-discovery, and the deep connection with the child's innate learning instincts must remain at the forefront.

The goal is to strive to strike a balance between Unschooling and formal schooling for different subjects. Celebrate the flexibility that Unschooling provides, embracing its essence while tailoring our approach to suit the unique needs and interests of our children.

Beyond the Testing

In Unschooling, the curriculum takes a backseat and learning unfolds organically. However for some, the question of testing arises. Does testing have a place in this curriculum-free learning environment? Allow me to shed light on this matter and delve into the essence of assessment within Unschooling.

In the world of Unschooling, the saying "the proof of the pudding is in the eating" holds true. Here, learning is not confined to sterile test papers or standardized assessments. Instead, it finds its roots in real-life experiences, where the practical application of knowledge becomes the ultimate test of understanding.

Imagine a child learning to bake a cake or carve a whistle from a bamboo stem. In Unschooling, there is no need for formal tests or evaluations. The true measure of learning lies in the joy of savoring the cake and the satisfaction of blowing the whistle. It is through these tangible outcomes that the mastery of skills and concepts is celebrated.

Unschooling recognizes that learning is not a mere accumulation of facts or regurgitation of information. It is a dynamic and holistic process that intertwines with everyday life. The focus shifts from test scores to the development of practical skills, critical thinking abilities, and a deep understanding of the subject matter.

In the absence of formal testing, Unschooling offers alternative avenues for assessment. Observations, conversations, and hands-on demonstrations become the markers of progress. Parents and mentors become keen observers, recognizing the growth and achievements of their Unschoolers through genuine engagement and meaningful conversations.

The essence of Unschooling lies in embracing the inherent joy of learning. It celebrates the unique strengths and passions of each individual, fostering a love for knowledge that extends far beyond the confines of traditional testing. In this vibrant tapestry of learning, assessment takes on a fluid and personalized form, tailored to the needs and interests of each learner.

If you choose Unschooling as the path for your child, you must learn to embrace a new paradigm of assessment within the realm of Unschooling. Move beyond the limitations of standardized tests and embrace the richness of real-world applications. You will need to forge a path where learning is not confined to test scores but flourishes through the embodiment of knowledge in practical and meaningful ways.

Power of Equitable Learning

The intricate dance between learning and authority unfolds within the realm of Unschooling, where the seeds of respect are sown in fertile soil. Unschooler children embark on a journey that shapes their understanding of authority, establishing a unique perspective rooted in equal partnership and mutual respect.

In the world of Unschooling, authority takes on a different meaning. It is not about dominance or control, but about wisdom, guidance, and earned respect. Unschooler children learn to discern the true essence of authority, recognizing that respect is not solely based on titles or appearances. Instead, it is earned through actions and character, a lesson they internalize through their educational experiences.

Throughout their educational journey, Unschooler children are treated with respect. Their parent-teachers serve as mentors and facilitators, valuing their thoughts, honoring their autonomy, and appreciating their ideas. In this nurturing environment of mutual respect, Unschoolers learn to appreciate and understand what genuine respect entails.

As they transition into adulthood, Unschoolers carry this profound understanding of authority with them. They possess the ability to discern when authority is earned, abused, or wielded with integrity. Their upbringing in an environment of equal partnership empowers them to navigate the complexities of authority figures, making conscious choices rooted in respect and discernment.

It is vital to dispel the misconception that Unschooler children grow up disrespecting authority or struggling with authority figures. On the contrary, they are more likely to extend respect to those who have truly earned it. Their journey of Unschooling instills within them an appreciation for the genuine qualities that merit respect—qualities that surpass titles, positions, and symbols of authority.

Within the realm of Unschooling, a generation of individuals is nurtured, embodying the essence of respect. They are empowered to question, challenge, and discern when authority aligns with their values. This delicate balance between Unschooling and authority cultivates compassionate, independent thinkers who navigate the world with integrity and discernment.

Embrace the transformative power of Unschooling, fostering a world where authority and respect intertwine harmoniously.

Professional Distance

The issue of professional distance in education raises thought-provoking questions about the role of parents as teachers in the Unschooling journey. Critics argue that parents should not homeschool their children for the same reason a pediatrician should not treat their own children. They suggest that professional distance is necessary for unbiased and effective education.

It is true that teacher-parents in Unschooling do not adhere to the conventional notion of professional distance found in traditional schooling environments. Instead, they foster a unique bond built on love, mutual respect, and kindness. They have the opportunity to intimately understand their child's strengths, weaknesses, interests, and inclinations. In the realm of Unschooling, this personal connection becomes a powerful catalyst for educational enrichment.

Unlike teachers in public schools who face time constraints and limited resources, parent-facilitators and learning partners in Unschooling can dedicate more focused and mindful attention to their child's learning journey. They have the flexibility to tailor education to their child's individual needs, providing a deeper level of engagement and support.

Unschooling values the whole child, nurturing not only their intellectual growth but also their emotional well-being. Parent-facilitators are uniquely positioned to provide a nurturing environment that fosters a love for learning, encourages critical thinking, and empowers their child to explore their passions and interests.

While concerns about professional distance may arise, it is important to recognize the immense value of the parent-child relationship in the Unschooling context. The bond of love and trust nurtured within the family sets a solid foundation for learning and growth. Parents become not only educators but also mentors, guides, and advocates for their child's educational journey.

In Unschooling, the emphasis is on providing children with a rich and diverse educational experience that goes beyond the confines of pre-determined curricula. It celebrates the uniqueness of each child, recognizing that true education extends far beyond the boundaries of a traditional classroom.

Ultimately, the decision to embrace Unschooling and take an active role in a child's education rests with the parents. It requires a deep commitment, dedication, and a belief in the power of familial bonds to nurture a lifelong love for learning.

So, while the concept of professional distance may hold significance in certain educational contexts, Unschooling celebrates the transformative role of parents as facilitators of their child's growth. It recognizes that the powerful connection between a parent and their child can foster an educational journey filled with wonder, curiosity, and meaningful discoveries.

In the realm of Unschooling, the parental role becomes a beacon of guidance, inspiration, and unwavering support, illuminating the path towards lifelong learning and personal fulfillment.

Unschooling and Special Needs

This is where the vast tapestry of human potential, unique abilities and diverse needs of every child intertwine. In Unschooling, we shatter the chains of limitation and embrace a holistic approach that celebrates the individuality of each and every child, regardless of their special needs.

Unschooling knows no bounds when it comes to the incredible journey of learning. Unlike the rigid confines of School, which often segregates and stigmatizes special-needs children, Unschooling welcomes them with open arms into a rich tapestry of inclusive education.

In School, the world is divided into neat categories of "typical," "average," and "ideal" children, leaving those with special needs feeling isolated and excluded. But Unschooling knows that every child is a masterpiece in their own right, deserving of an education that nurtures their unique strengths and challenges.

Within the nurturing embrace of Unschooling, children of all abilities, be it physical, cognitive, or emotional, find themselves in the company of a diverse community. No longer confined to a remedial group or segregated classroom, they are free to interact with peers of different ages, interests, and abilities. This rich tapestry of inclusion becomes the fertile ground for growth, empathy, and understanding.

Unschooling understands that the true beauty of education lies in the tapestry of human connection. By fostering an environment where children of diverse abilities coexist, learn from one another, and celebrate their differences, we create a harmonious symphony of learning and growth.

You may wonder if Unschooling can meet the unique needs of children with special needs. Rest assured, for Unschooling is not bound by preconceived notions of an ideal child or fixed expectations. It embraces the individuality of each child, providing the freedom to learn at their own pace, in their own way.

Unschooling is a pathway that honors the inherent worth and potential of every child, embracing their unique abilities and challenges. By creating an environment that fosters inclusion and celebrates diversity, Unschooling becomes a beacon of hope and opportunity for children with special needs.

In this remarkable journey, parents and caregivers play a vital role as guides and facilitators. They navigate the ever-changing landscape of their child's growth, offering support, resources, and a nurturing presence. Together, they embark on an odyssey of discovery, unlocking the hidden treasures within each child's heart.

Remember that Unschooling is not a one-size-fits-all solution, but a philosophy that embraces the individuality of each child. It requires flexibility, adaptability, and a deep understanding of your child's unique needs. Seek out resources, connect with support networks, and trust in your intuition as you navigate this extraordinary journey.

Fear not the path of Unschooling for children with special needs. Embrace the boundless possibilities that lie within the nurturing embrace of this approach. Unschooling creates a world where every child, regardless of their abilities, can thrive, learn, and celebrate their unique place in the tapestry of education.

Chapter 9 – Higher Education

College Admissions

How do Unschoolers navigate the path to college admission? It's a question that often arises, and the answer lies in the recognition that Unschoolers embark on a similar journey as their Schooler counterparts. The road to college is paved with familiar steps: transcript submissions, entrance exam preparations, and the art of crafting compelling essays. Unschoolers, just like their peers, understand the importance of meeting the specific requirements set forth by their chosen colleges and universities.

While the methods may differ, the underlying principles remain the same. Unschoolers approach the college application process with a unique perspective, showcasing their diverse educational experiences and personal growth. They highlight their intellectual curiosity, their self-directed learning journeys, and the valuable skills they have cultivated outside the traditional classroom walls.

The beauty of Unschooling lies in its ability to nurture a deep sense of individuality and a genuine love for learning. Unschoolers, armed with a diverse set of experiences and a thirst for knowledge, embark on their college application journey with confidence and enthusiasm. They are not confined by rigid academic structures but instead flourish in the freedom to explore their passions, develop critical thinking skills, and pursue meaningful projects that align with their interests.

It is important to remember that each college and university sets its own admission procedures. Unschoolers, like Schoolers, adapt to the requirements of the institutions they wish to attend. They showcase their unique educational paths, highlighting their accomplishments, experiences, and personal growth. Through thoughtful presentation and genuine self-expression, Unschoolers make their mark and demonstrate their readiness for higher education.

In the realm of college admissions, Unschoolers prove that their educational journey, marked by curiosity, self-motivation, and a love for learning, prepares them to thrive in the academic environment. Their ability to showcase their holistic development and demonstrate their readiness for higher education opens doors to a myriad of opportunities.

Fear not the college application process. Unschoolers, armed with their distinctive educational narratives and a passion for learning, embark on this exciting journey, ready to leave their mark on the world of academia. With each step they take, they exemplify the power of Unschooling and inspire others to embrace the transformative potential of education outside the confines of traditional schooling.

Certification

In the realm of homeschooling and Unschooling, the question arises: should certification be a requirement for those who embark on this educational path? Unschooling philosophy vehemently rejects the notion as undemocratic and counter to the very essence of true education. It stands firm in its belief that anyone possessing skill or knowledge has the inherent right to share it with others, unburdened by the need for official approval.

The pioneers of Unschooling, known as the Deschoolers, emphasize the significance of connecting children with the real world and its practitioners. They advocate for exposing young minds to ordinary individuals who excel in their crafts, be it skilled workmen, welders, or car mechanics. These practitioners, or as John Holt beautifully describes them, the "do-ers," offer invaluable insights and practical wisdom that textbooks and standardized curricula fail to capture.

John Gatto, a passionate advocate for alternative education, boldly declares that nothing truly useful is learned within the confines of traditional schooling. He challenges us to question our own experiences and realize that the knowledge and skills we deem valuable were acquired beyond the confines of compulsory time spent under the guidance of certified educators. Gatto goes even further, urging us to break free from the monopoly of teacher certification. He believes that true education should be accessible to all, and anyone with something valuable to teach should have the opportunity to do so. This, he asserts, is a matter of utmost importance.

The call to liberate knowledge from the shackles of certification resonates deeply within the Unschooling community. It recognizes that expertise and wisdom can come from various sources, not just from those endorsed by institutional credentials. Unschooling celebrates the diversity of teachers and embraces the notion that valuable lessons can be learned from individuals who may not possess official certification but possess a wealth of practical experience and a genuine passion for sharing their knowledge.

In the realm of Unschooling, the certification requirement fades away, making room for a dynamic and inclusive educational landscape. It empowers individuals to teach and learn from one another, fostering a rich tapestry of knowledge exchange that extends far beyond the confines of traditional schooling. In this liberating environment, the pursuit of knowledge becomes a collaborative journey, where everyone's unique expertise is honored and celebrated.

So, let us challenge the notion of certification and embrace the freedom to teach. By breaking down the barriers that confine knowledge and by recognizing the value of diverse voices, we unlock the true potential of education and pave the way for a more vibrant and inclusive learning experience for all.

Catalyst for University Education

The scope of Unschooling extends far beyond the realm of primary and secondary education; it reaches into the very fabric of our society, challenging the established norms that govern the higher education landscape. Unschoolers contend that before we address the question of university education, we must first confront the formidable adversary that is 'School' itself—a system that poses a grave threat to the holistic development of our children and the preservation of our cherished individual liberties.

John Gatto, a staunch critic of standardized, state-imposed schooling, emphasizes the criticality of the early years, particularly between grade one and grade three. It is during this formative period that the School system systematically extinguishes a child's innate love for learning, stifling their natural curiosity and enthusiasm. Unschoolers recognize that in order to liberate our children's potential, we must dismantle the oppressive machinery of School that suffocates their intellectual growth.

The landscape of universities, however, presents a distinct paradigm. These institutions operate within a marketplace for higher education, subject to regulatory frameworks. Unlike primary and secondary schooling, university attendance is not compulsory. As such, universities find themselves in a position where they must respond and adapt to the emergence of a significant cohort of Unschooled individuals who may seek enrollment.

In the face of this shifting educational landscape, universities may be compelled to reevaluate their structures, pedagogical approaches, and admission criteria. The rise of Unschooling creates a demand for educational experiences that align with the values of self-directed learning, individual autonomy, and a rejection of standardized curricula. Universities, in order to attract and accommodate this emerging wave of Unschooled students, may be prompted to revamp their offerings and provide more flexible, learner-centric pathways.

While the impact of Unschooling on university education remains to be fully realized, the potential for change is evident. As the number of Unschooled individuals pursuing higher education grows, universities will inevitably face the need to adapt to this evolving landscape. The advent of a new generation of learners, unencumbered by the shackles of traditional schooling, holds the potential to reshape the very foundations of higher education.

In this transformative journey, Unschooling serves as a catalyst, challenging the status quo and paving the way for a more diverse, flexible, and inclusive approach to university education. As Unschoolers continue to carve their path, universities must recognize the changing tides and seize the opportunity to reimagine their role in nurturing the intellectual and personal growth of these unique individuals.

So, while Unschooling's immediate focus lies in dismantling the barriers imposed by traditional schooling, its ripple effects are far-reaching. It calls upon universities to adapt, evolve, and embrace the shifting educational landscape, ensuring that the ideals of self-directed learning and personal autonomy are not confined to the early years but extend to the realm of higher education. Together, Unschooling and universities can shape a future where the pursuit of knowledge is driven by passion, curiosity, and a relentless quest for personal and intellectual growth.

Unschooling Applicants

As the number of Unschooler applicants steadily rises, the question arises: How are universities responding to this transformative shift in learning practices?

While we have yet to reach a critical mass of Unschooled individuals, progress is undeniably underway. However, it is crucial to recognize that the bulk of the work lies in reforming primary and secondary education, laying the foundation for a more profound impact on the post-secondary sector.

Encouragingly, there are early indications that certain universities are embracing the winds of change and showing a willingness to accommodate non-traditional learners, including the Unschooled. These institutions recognize the value of opening their doors to a diverse range of applicants, valuing unique learning journeys and unconventional educational paths.

The advent of Massive Open Onlinc Courses (MOOCs) has contributed to this shift, with prominent institutions such as MIT making their learning resources available online. This accessibility allows Unschooled individuals to access high-quality educational materials, broadening their horizons and expanding their knowledge base beyond the confines of traditional schooling.

While these developments signal a promising direction, we are still in the early stages of the transformation. It will take time and continued advocacy for Unschooling principles to permeate the broader educational landscape. However, the seeds of change have been sown, and the future holds great potential for a more inclusive, learner-centric approach to higher education.

As Unschooling gains momentum and more individuals embark on this path of self-directed learning, universities will inevitably feel the pressure to adapt and respond to the evolving educational landscape. The success stories of Unschooled applicants who thrive in university settings will serve as powerful testaments to the effectiveness and validity of this alternative approach.

It is an exciting time for both Unschoolers and universities as we navigate this shifting educational paradigm. Together, we can shape a future where institutions of higher learning embrace diversity, flexibility, and the pursuit of knowledge driven by intrinsic motivation and passion. The journey is just beginning, and as we forge ahead, we must remain steadfast in our commitment to fostering an educational environment that honors the autonomy and individuality of each learner.

So, while the impact of Unschooling on university admissions is still unfolding, the signs of change are encouraging. As more institutions recognize the value of non-traditional learning experiences, we inch closer to a future where Unschooling applicants are not only acknowledged but celebrated for their unique perspectives, intellectual curiosity, and self-directed growth.

Together, Unschoolers and universities can embark on a remarkable journey of transformation, where education is liberated from the confines of tradition and embraces the boundless possibilities of self-discovery and personal growth. The future of Unschooling applicants is a testament to the power of choice, autonomy, and the unyielding spirit of exploration.

The College Conundrum

When it comes to the question of whether Unschoolers should pursue a college education, there is no one-size-fits-all answer. It is an individual choice that ultimately rests upon the aspirations and circumstances of each Unschooled young person. However, Unschoolers possess a unique advantage when it comes to making this decision—one that sets them apart from others.

Unschooling equips young individuals with the essential skills of independent thinking, self-motivation, and self-direction. It instills a deep sense of curiosity and a thirst for knowledge that goes beyond the boundaries of traditional education. By embracing the freedom to explore their passions and interests,

Unschoolers develop a level of self-awareness and purpose that sets them on a distinct path.

While college or university can be a valuable learning resource, it is essential to recognize the changing landscape of higher education. The university system itself is undergoing a transformation, grappling with the need to retain its prestige, authority, and monopoly on knowledge. In response, forward-thinking institutions are adopting innovative strategies, such as offering Massive Open Online Courses (MOOCs) and providing access to online course materials. The impact and effectiveness of these approaches are still unfolding, and time will reveal their true value.

In the meantime, Unschoolers have a vast array of learning resources at their disposal, both within and beyond the confines of a traditional college setting. The walls of a university are no longer the sole gatekeepers of knowledge. Libraries, online platforms, mentorships, internships, and apprenticeships present opportunities for an 18-year-old Unschooler to satiate their interests and pursue their ambitions.

Unschoolers are poised to embrace a different kind of education—one that transcends the confines of a degree and focuses on lifelong learning and personal growth. They have the freedom to curate their educational journey, seeking experiences and knowledge that align with their unique goals and aspirations.

While the decision to pursue a college education remains a personal one, Unschoolers possess a distinct advantage. Their unconventional upbringing has nurtured a spirit of intellectual curiosity, adaptability, and self-determination. Armed with these qualities, they are well-equipped to navigate the ever-changing educational landscape and forge their own path towards personal and professional fulfillment.

So, should Unschoolers go to college when they reach college-going age? The answer lies within the heart and mind of each individual. It is a decision that should be made with careful consideration, weighing the available options and aligning with personal aspirations. Whether it be through traditional academia or alternative avenues, the key is to continue embracing the spirit of lifelong learning and never cease the pursuit of knowledge.

Crafting the College Application

The prospect of putting together a college admissions application as an Unschooler may seem daunting at first glance. After all, the Unschooling journey is characterized by its unique approach to education, driven by individual interests and self-directed learning. But fear not, for with thoughtful planning and foresight, an Unschooler can indeed assemble a compelling application that paves the way to college acceptance.

It is important to note that this hinges upon whether college has been a long-standing goal or a potential avenue that has remained open throughout the Unschooling journey. If higher education has been part of the vision from the outset, then it requires strategic foresight and intentional steps to position oneself for success.

The key lies in recognizing that shaping a college application is not a last-minute endeavor. It necessitates a thoughtful approach from the very beginning. Unschoolers must actively plan and curate their learning experiences to align with the expectations and requirements of colleges and universities.

Building a robust college application as an Unschooler involves a multifaceted approach. It goes beyond mere academic achievements and standardized test scores. Unschoolers have the unique opportunity to showcase their unconventional educational journey, emphasizing their intellectual curiosity, self-motivation, and passion for learning. This can be done through various avenues such as:

Documentation of Learning: Keeping a portfolio or journal that chronicles the Unschooling journey, highlighting significant projects, research, and independent studies. This serves as tangible evidence of intellectual growth and personal development.

Pursuing Passionate Interests: Unschoolers have the freedom to delve deeply into their passions. Showcasing substantial accomplishments in areas of interest through internships, community service, creative projects, or entrepreneurial ventures can make a compelling case for admission.

Collaborative Learning Experiences: Engaging in collaborative projects, participating in community organizations, or seeking mentorships and apprenticeships can demonstrate social skills, teamwork, and a commitment to making a positive impact beyond the traditional classroom setting.

Seeking External Validation: Participating in standardized tests, earning industry certifications, or enrolling in college-level courses can provide external validation of academic abilities and enhance the overall application.

It is essential to approach the college application process with a growth mindset and a willingness to advocate for oneself. Unschoolers must be prepared to articulate their educational journey, highlighting the unique strengths and qualities they have developed along the way. Authenticity, self-reflection, and a clear sense of purpose will set an Unschooler's application apart from the rest.

While the Unschooling approach may be unconventional, colleges and universities are increasingly recognizing the value of diverse educational paths. They are seeking students who bring a fresh perspective, intellectual curiosity, and a drive to make a difference in the world. Unschoolers have the opportunity to showcase these qualities, illustrating how their self-directed learning has prepared them for success in higher education.

So, can an Unschooler put together a college admissions application that will be accepted? Absolutely. It requires careful planning, intentional experiences, and a thoughtful presentation of one's unique educational journey. With these ingredients, an Unschooler can confidently navigate the college admissions process, paving the way for a future brimming with possibilities.

Notes into Transcript

When it comes to crafting a college transcript for an Unschooler, the process may seem unconventional at first. But fear not, for with careful consideration and creative ingenuity, parents can seamlessly transform their meticulously kept notes into a captivating masterpiece.

The first step is to gather all the notes, journals, and records that have been diligently maintained throughout the educational journey. These invaluable resources will form the foundation of the transcript, painting a vivid picture of the Unschooler's academic pursuits and personal growth.

Now comes the task of weaving these diverse learning experiences into a cohesive transcript.

Unschooling embraces both traditional and nontraditional approaches to education, and the transcript should reflect this rich tapestry. Parents must skillfully showcase a balance of conventional subject matter while highlighting the unique nontraditional studies their child has passionately pursued.

In the realm of Unschooling, every learning adventure is an opportunity to delve into various disciplines. For example, a five-year exploration of fly fishing can be elegantly categorized under the umbrella of "science." Parents can delve into the realms of ichthyology, physics, and entomology, showcasing how this captivating pursuit extends beyond mere hobby into a multifaceted academic journey. However, it is essential to curate the material thoughtfully, excluding any extraneous information that may distract from the core narrative.

For Unschoolers with a passion for the arts, visual artists, photographers, potters, dancers, actors, singers, and musicians, there is an additional dimension to consider. Alongside the transcript, they have the opportunity to assemble a captivating portfolio, video, or audio tape showcasing their remarkable talents. These artistic expressions serve as a visual and auditory testament to their dedication, creativity, and growth as artists, providing a powerful complement to the written transcript.

As the final strokes are added to the transcript, it is important to present the Unschooler's journey in a format that resonates with college admissions boards. While remaining authentic to the Unschooling philosophy, parents may choose to incorporate traditional subject headings into the transcript. This strategic decision helps admissions officers recognize the breadth and depth of the Unschooler's studies, providing a familiar framework for evaluation.

The process of transforming notes into a college transcript is an art form in itself. It requires careful curation, thoughtful categorization, and a keen eye for capturing the essence of the Unschooler's educational odyssey. Each transcript becomes a masterpiece, showcasing the unique blend of passion, intellectual curiosity, and personal growth that defines the Unschooling experience.

Dear Unschooling parents, embrace this opportunity to present your child's journey with artistry and eloquence. Let your transcript become a canvas, where colors of knowledge, creativity, and self-discovery intertwine to create a masterpiece that showcases the Unschooler's remarkable academic and personal growth.

So, gather your notes, infuse them with creativity, and allow the transcript to become a testament to the power of Unschooling—a testament that captures the spirit of intellectual exploration, independence, and the unwavering pursuit of knowledge that define the Unschooler's educational journey.

Crafting the College Transcript

As an Unschooler or a parent of an Unschooler, the task of preparing a transcript for a college admissions application may initially seem perplexing. But fear not, for there are practical steps you can take to create a comprehensive and compelling record of your child's educational journey.

First and foremost, it is essential to start documenting learning interests and activities early on, ideally during the early teen years. Waiting until the so-called "high school years" may result in overlooking significant information that could greatly benefit your child's college transcript. By establishing a system for documenting learning from the outset, you ensure that no valuable experiences or achievements slip through the cracks.

One approach is to utilize a loose-leaf ring binder for each child. This serves as a flexible and accessible repository for recording their educational journey. Whenever a noteworthy learning experience arises, whether it be on a daily, weekly, biweekly, or monthly basis, make a note on a new punched page. This system allows you to capture the entirety of your child's learning, providing a comprehensive perspective for college admissions.

For recurring activities that form a significant part of your child's educational journey, such as regular club participation or community service commitments, list them once with their duration. This prevents unnecessary repetition while still showcasing the depth and consistency of their engagement. For more specific accomplishments, such as securing a leading part in a play, a solo performance, or winning a prize, be sure to include those notable details as well.

As you gather your notes, it is essential to compile them into a coherent and organized sequence on a regular basis. Some parents find that a timeframe of every 4 to 6 months works well for this purpose. Regularly updating and refining the transcript ensures that it accurately reflects your child's evolving educational journey.

When it comes to structuring the transcript, you may find it helpful to incorporate both traditional academic subject headings and personalized descriptors. While this may go against the grain of Unschooling's organic and holistic approach to education, it provides a recognizable framework for college admissions officers. Start with familiar headings like English, Science, Social Studies, and Math, and augment them with additional subject headings that aptly capture the unique learning experiences your child has embraced.

Remember, your goal is to create a transcript that reflects the rich tapestry of your child's education, showcasing their intellectual growth, personal development, and pursuit of their passions. It is an opportunity to demonstrate their self-directed learning, critical thinking abilities, and the breadth and depth of their knowledge.

Crafting a compelling college transcript for an Unschooler requires intentionality, attention to detail, and a commitment to showcasing the diverse and dynamic educational journey your child has embarked upon. Embrace the opportunity to tell their unique story, illustrating their intellectual curiosity, self-motivation, and the remarkable ways in which they have cultivated their passions and pursued knowledge.

In the realm of Unschooling, the college transcript becomes a testament to the power of self-directed learning, demonstrating that education flourishes when it is driven by genuine interest, personal autonomy, and a love for lifelong learning.

So fear not, dear Unschooler, for you have the tools to create a compelling college transcript that illuminates your educational journey. Embrace the opportunity to showcase your unique path, and let your transcript become a reflection of the remarkable learning experiences that have shaped you into the curious, independent, and intellectually vibrant individual you are today.

Journey to College

The misconception persists—that Unschoolers, who have never experienced the constraints of a traditional school, might struggle to cope with the rigors of a college environment. Allow me, my curious reader, to dispel this myth and shed light on the remarkable adaptability and readiness of Unschoolers as they embark on their higher education journey.

It is true that Unschoolers thrive in an environment that values freedom, self-direction, and a fluid approach to learning. However, let us not overlook the fact that their lives are rich with structure, organization, and activities that require adherence to deadlines and schedules. Just like anyone else, they catch buses, make calls, meet people at designated times and places, and even engage in online interactions—all within the framework of their own self-motivation.

The secret lies in the intrinsic motivation that propels Unschoolers forward. They have embraced structured activities and organized endeavors not out of obligation, but because they genuinely wanted to. Their entire educational journey has been driven by their passion, curiosity, and thirst for knowledge. Therefore, when faced with the college lecture-timetable and supervision meetings with professors, Unschoolers are more than prepared to excel.

Imagine a classroom where every student is there by choice, fully engaged and eager to participate. That is the reality of an Unschooler in college. Their attendance is not a mere obligation; it is a conscious decision fueled by their genuine desire to be present and actively participate in the learning process. This intrinsic motivation becomes their guiding force, propelling them to embrace each class, seize every opportunity, and unlock their full potential.

Unschoolers have honed the skills of time management, self-discipline, and self-motivation throughout their educational journey. They possess the resilience and adaptability necessary to thrive in a structured college environment. Their experiences of learning under their own volition have instilled in them a deep sense of responsibility and a drive to make the most of every educational opportunity that comes their way.

The Unschooler enters the college landscape with an open mind, a thirst for knowledge, and a commitment to make the most of every educational opportunity that comes their way. They stand tall, ready to embrace the challenges, forge connections with professors and fellow students, and leave an indelible mark on their educational journey.

Unschoolers bring with them a vibrant spirit, an unwavering passion for learning, and a readiness to embrace the structured environment of college. With their unique approach to education, they are poised to thrive, excel, and make a lasting impact. The college lecture hall becomes a stage upon which they unleash their boundless curiosity, fuel their intellectual growth, and contribute to the vibrant tapestry of academia.

You can rest assured that the Unschooler is more than equipped to navigate the constraints of a college environment. Their unique path has prepared them to embrace structure, engage in meaningful interactions, and excel in their academic pursuits. With their intrinsic motivation and unwavering determination, the Unschooler is ready to make their mark on the world of higher education.

Path to The Ivy Leagues

Are Unschoolers accepted in the top Ivy League universities or just in State colleges or Community colleges? Let me assure you, my friend, that the doors to academic excellence are not closed to those who embrace the path of Unschooling. In fact, prestigious institutions such as Harvard, Brown, Princeton, Yale, and Stanford have opened their gates to homeschoolers, including the vibrant community of Unschoolers.

Gone are the days when Unschooling was met with skepticism and doubt. Society is evolving, and with it, so are the perceptions surrounding alternative education. Universities and admissions committees are becoming increasingly open-minded, recognizing the unique advantages that Unschoolers bring to the table. Your child, my dear reader, has the opportunity to showcase their unconventional educational journey as a testament to their drive, resourcefulness, and real-world experiences.

While traditional academic achievements like test scores and transcripts still hold value, Unschoolers have the distinct advantage of being able to demonstrate their practical skills, work experience, apprenticeships, and self-directed study. They can showcase a portfolio that goes beyond grades and showcases their authentic growth, intellectual pursuits, and hands-on exploration. These attributes set them apart from the sea of applicants and reveal a depth of knowledge and a passion for learning that traditional schooling often fails to capture.

Unschooling nurtures a sense of independence, critical thinking, and self-motivation—the very qualities that top universities value in their prospective students. By embracing the freedom to pursue their interests and curiosities, Unschoolers develop a unique perspective on the world and cultivate a thirst for knowledge that extends far beyond the boundaries of a traditional classroom.

So, rest assured that the path to higher education is not limited for Unschoolers. The journey may be unconventional, but it is one filled with opportunities to showcase their remarkable potential, stand out from the crowd, and prove that true education knows no boundaries. As the paradigm shifts and universities embrace the changing landscape of education, Unschoolers find themselves welcomed into the hallowed halls of academic excellence, ready to make their mark on the world.

The UnCollege Movement

Let me introduce you to a remarkable movement that has been challenging the very notion of college education since its emergence in 2010: UnCollege. At its core, UnCollege seeks to debunk the belief that a college degree is essential for success in life, careers, entrepreneurship, and all other endeavors. It boldly asserts that college, as we know it, is a redundant institution, lacking relevance in today's rapidly evolving world.

What makes UnCollege even more intriguing is that it was initiated by a young man named Dale J. Stephens, who himself had experienced the power of Unschooling firsthand. Dale serves as a living testament to the possibilities that emerge when one dares to question the traditional paths to success and forge their own unique journey.

Since its inception, UnCollege has steadily gained influence, momentum, and traction. It serves as a logical extension of the Unschooling philosophy, pushing the boundaries of what education means and challenging the established norms. While UnCollege recognizes the importance of self-directed learning and real-world experiences, its primary focus is on the reevaluation of higher education in later stages of life.

The significance of the UnCollege Movement cannot be understated. It has sparked a much-needed conversation about the purpose and value of traditional university education. By questioning the necessity of a college degree, UnCollege forces us to reexamine the assumptions we hold about the linear progression from high school to college to career. It invites us to explore alternative paths and unconventional approaches to personal and professional growth.

While UnCollege complements the principles of Unschooling, it is important to acknowledge that the heart of Unschooling lies in the formative years of education. However, UnCollege expands the discourse by challenging the status quo of higher education and encouraging individuals to critically evaluate their choices.

To delve deeper into the UnCollege Movement and explore its fascinating ideas, I recommend visiting www.UnCollege.org. There, you will find a wealth of resources, testimonials, and thought-provoking insights that shed light on this revolutionary movement.

In a world where the definition of success is being redefined, UnCollege stands at the forefront, urging us to question the traditional narratives of education and pursue alternative paths that align with our unique aspirations and passions. It invites us to imagine a future where learning is not confined within the walls of a university but is a lifelong pursuit fueled by curiosity, experience, and the desire to make a meaningful impact.

The significance of UnCollege lies in its ability to challenge the status quo, spark dialogue, and inspire individuals to carve their own paths to success. It serves as a powerful reminder that education is not confined to the walls of an institution but is a transformative journey that can be shaped and customized according to one's own dreams and aspirations.

Chapter 10 – The Future Is Now

The Power of Technology in Unschooling

In the realm of Unschooling, technology serves as a catalyst for success, enabling learners to break free from the passive learning experiences ingrained within traditional schooling systems. It empowers Unschoolers to embrace an active and self-directed approach to education, unlocking a world of possibilities and opportunities.

Unlike the structured and rigid nature of traditional schooling, Unschooling learners are free to harness technology in transformative ways. They can embark on ambitious projects, such as creating their own websites, dedicating days or even weeks to refine their digital creations. With uninterrupted focus and dedication, they can delve into web research on topics that ignite their curiosity, immersing themselves in a realm of knowledge without the constraints of a school bell dictating their learning pace.

One of the greatest advantages of technology for Unschoolers is the ability to connect and communicate with like-minded learners from around the world. Through blogs and online forums, they can engage in vibrant discussions, share ideas, and seek assistance when needed. Whether it's seeking guidance from fellow learners or reaching out to world experts, technology fosters a sense of collaboration and community that transcends geographical boundaries.

Online forums become havens of support, where Unschoolers can seek help, information, and advice on any issue or challenge they encounter. They become active participants in a dynamic exchange of knowledge, gaining valuable insights and expanding their horizons.

Technology not only facilitates the acquisition of information and knowledge but also nurtures a sense of self-esteem and confidence in Unschoolers. When they can be the ones providing guidance and support to fellow learners, their expertise and contributions are valued and celebrated. This affirmation strengthens their belief in their own abilities and reinforces their sense of worth as active contributors to the learning community.

In the realm of Unschooling, technology becomes a powerful ally, propelling learners towards success and self-actualization. It provides a platform for creativity, exploration, and connection that amplifies the educational experience beyond the confines of a traditional classroom.

However, it is important to recognize that technology is a tool, and its effective use in Unschooling relies on the guidance and mentorship of parents. They play an essential role in fostering responsible digital citizenship, ensuring that technology is used in a balanced and purposeful manner.

By embracing the power of technology, Unschoolers unlock a world of endless possibilities, where learning knows no boundaries. It is a testament to the limitless potential of the human mind, the transformative nature of personalized education, and the boundless opportunities that technology presents on the journey of Unschooling success.

Embracing the Internet in Unschooling

In the realm of Unschooling, the Internet has become an invaluable tool, opening up a vast world of knowledge and resources for students who choose to learn outside of traditional schooling. It has revolutionized the way we access information, connect with others, and embark on our personal learning journeys.

While not essential for Unschooling, the Internet has emerged as a powerful enabler, providing unparalleled opportunities for independent, self-directed learning. Through online platforms and resources, Unschoolers can delve into a wide range of subjects, explore diverse perspectives, and engage in meaningful discussions with individuals from around the globe.

The Internet's social communication dimension, often referred to as Web 2.0, has transformed the vision put forth by visionary thinkers like Ivan Illich in the early 1970s. Illich envisioned a world where individuals could freely and directly share knowledge, bypassing the filters and control structures of institutionalized education. Today, that vision has become a reality, with Unschoolers embracing the democratizing power of the Internet to learn from and collaborate with others on a peer-to-peer basis.

One remarkable example of the Internet's impact on Unschooling is highlighted in Will Richardson's thought-provoking book, "*Why School? How Education Must Change When Learning and Information Are Everywhere.*" Richardson shares an inspiring story that exemplifies the seamless integration of technology and self-directed learning in today's Unschooling landscape.

The Internet has empowered Unschoolers to curate their own learning experiences, leveraging a vast array of digital resources, online courses, virtual communities, and interactive platforms. It transcends the limitations of physical classrooms, offering flexibility, customization, and a wealth of learning opportunities tailored to each student's unique interests and aspirations.

However, it is important to approach the Internet with discernment and critical thinking skills, guiding children to navigate the digital landscape responsibly and safely. Unschooling parents play an active role in fostering digital literacy, helping their children develop the skills to evaluate information, engage in meaningful online interactions, and navigate the vast sea of knowledge with a discerning eye.

In the realm of Unschooling, the Internet is not just a tool; it is a gateway to boundless knowledge, diverse perspectives, and collaborative learning. It amplifies the voices of learners, connecting them with a global community of fellow explorers. As technology continues to evolve, the Internet will undoubtedly play an even more significant role in the Unschooling movement, enriching the educational experiences of students and empowering them to shape their own learning paths.

I say, let's embrace the power of the web, leveraging its vast resources and connectivity to embark on a journey of self-directed learning and discovery. In the digital age, the Internet is not only transforming education but also redefining what it means to be a lifelong learner.

Curiosity and Mentorship

As we ponder the role of teachers in an ever-changing educational landscape, the question arises: What skills will future teachers need? In this vision of a transformed learning environment, the answer takes an intriguing turn.

In this brave new world, teachers will rely not on conventional training or formal certifications, but rather on the richness of their life experiences and the genuine skills they have acquired along their unique paths. Gone are the rigid notions of a prescribed curriculum or standardized assessments. Instead, teachers will draw upon their diverse expertise, be it building a house, sailing a boat, or mastering the art of wilderness survival.

However, it is important to note that the skill set required goes far beyond practical craftsmanship. While the ability to navigate the intricacies of mathematics, science, and other academic disciplines will still hold value, the true essence of future teachers lies in their ability to inspire, nurture curiosity, and act as mentors.

In this transformative landscape, teachers will serve as guides and facilitators, encouraging their students to delve into the depths of their interests and passions. Mentoring will be at the heart of their role, connecting students with professionals and experts in various fields.

Imagine a future where a budding physicist finds mentorship from a renowned scientist, a passionate entrepreneur receives guidance from a seasoned business mogul, or a curious mind explores the wonders of astronomy under the wing of an astrophysicist. These mentorship relationships will foster not only the acquisition of knowledge but also the cultivation of critical thinking, creativity, and problem-solving skills.

Future teachers will possess the art of weaving connections, cultivating an environment where learning transcends the boundaries of a traditional classroom. They will embrace the role of a lifelong learner themselves, continuously seeking new knowledge and staying abreast of emerging discoveries.

While the precise nature of these skills may be subject to speculation, one thing remains certain: future teachers will be masters of inspiration, fostering an environment where the flame of curiosity burns bright, and the joy of learning becomes a lifelong pursuit.

In this dynamic educational paradigm, teachers will be catalysts for growth, guiding students towards a deeper understanding of themselves and the world around them. Through their mentorship, they will unlock the vast potential within each learner, nurturing a generation of thinkers, innovators, and seekers of truth.

So, as we peer into the horizon of education's future, let us remember that the skills of future teachers go beyond textbooks and examinations. They lie in the ability to ignite a spark, ignite a passion, and guide the next generation towards a limitless world of possibilities.

The Evolution of Democracy

In the fascinating realm of Unschooling, a remarkable transformation occurs in our perception of authority. The traditional belief in the unquestionable need for authority, the psychology of master and slave, is challenged and ultimately transcended.

Unschooling, with its emphasis on independent learning and self-direction, dismisses the notion of hierarchical power structures. The chains of obedience to authority are replaced by the liberation of individual judgment and critical thinking. Conformity, that stifling force that demands uniformity, gives way to vibrant discussions that pave the path towards consensus.

In this enlightened paradigm, the worship of authority figures becomes obsolete. Instead, a new foundation is laid—one built upon the principles of equality, partnership, mutual respect, and the recognition of each individual's intrinsic worth.

Unschooling, especially when applied in the education of young minds, becomes the catalyst for the birth of a profound democracy. It nurtures the seeds of autonomy, fostering the growth of individuals capable of independent thought and active participation in the shaping of society.

But what does this mean for the concept of authority itself? In the interconnected digital age, the wisdom of the crowd and the web's mechanisms for forming opinions, judgments, and evaluations gain prominence. The power dynamics shift, and the voice of each individual resonates within the collective consciousness.

Gone are the days when authority was unquestioned, when the few held sway over the many. Unschooling, with its commitment to self-directed learning and exploration, empowers individuals to question, challenge, and seek truth for themselves. It instills the belief that knowledge is not something bestowed by an authoritative figure, but rather something to be discovered, shared, and continuously expanded upon.

As Unschooling weaves its magic, the old belief in authority dissipates, making way for a blossoming democracy where the wisdom of the crowd, grounded in the principles of dialogue and mutual respect, becomes the driving force behind decision-making and collective progress.

So, in the realm of Unschooling, the liberation of authority emerges as a transformative force. It opens doors to a future where power is distributed, where the voices of all individuals, connected and engaged, shape the fabric of our society. It is through this profound shift in mindset that Unschooling not only revolutionizes education but also becomes an agent of social change—a beacon guiding us towards a more democratic and equitable world.

The Possibility of Unschooling's Fate

Ah, the ever-present question of failure. Could Unschooling, this noble and high-minded idea, stumble and end up in the annals of forgotten endeavors? It is a possibility, indeed. History is filled with concepts that once held promise but were eventually discarded. However, let us not dwell on the negative but instead embrace a more hopeful perspective.

We yearn for Unschooling to thrive and evolve, to defy the odds and leave an indelible mark on the educational landscape. There is something inherently captivating about this approach—it is simple yet profound, offering a new paradigm for learning. And the best part? Anyone can embark on this journey.

The success of Unschooling lies not only in its principles but also in the hands of those who dare to embrace it. Each individual who wholeheartedly embraces Unschooling becomes a vital contributor to its growth and prosperity. It is a collaborative effort, fueled by the passion and dedication of parents, caregivers, and the wider community.

So, my dear reader, the question arises: Could you be a part of this transformative movement? Could you, with an open heart and a willingness to challenge conventional norms, embark on the Unschooling path? The answer lies within you. Unschooling calls upon the brave, the curious, and the seekers of alternative educational experiences.

Unschooling may face obstacles and skepticism along the way, but it is our collective responsibility to nurture and cultivate its potential. Let us envision a future where Unschooling not only survives but thrives, empowering generations to come.

In this grand tapestry of education, we have the power to shape the narrative. Will Unschooling stand the test of time, or will it fade into obscurity? The choice is ours to make. Embrace the possibility, embark on the journey, and together let us weave a legacy that ignites the minds and hearts of learners for generations to come.

Glimpse into a Deschooled Future

Peering into the crystal ball of the future, we find ourselves in a realm of speculation. No one can truly predict what lies ahead. However, let us indulge in the realm of possibility and envision one potential scenario: a future where Unschooling flourishes and ultimately eclipses the traditional educational system we currently have.

In this hypothetical future, the notion of traditional Schools as we know them today would fade away. Instead, a Deschooled society would emerge, closely resembling the captivating vision portrayed in Ivan Illich's seminal work, "Deschooling Society."

Under the banner of Unschooling, children's education would predominantly take place within the nurturing embrace of their own homes and families. Meanwhile, the once-familiar School buildings would undergo a profound transformation. No longer housing structured classrooms and rigid curricula, these buildings would find new purpose as vibrant spaces for dynamic peer-to-peer learning, engaging discussions, and creative exchanges.

Illich eloquently lamented the scarcity of suitable environments for the kind of democratic, non-credentialed learning interactions he envisioned. In this imagined future, the very buildings that once encapsulated the traditional educational system would be reclaimed and repurposed to fulfill Illich's dream.

As we ponder this vision of a Deschooled society, it is crucial to acknowledge that the future remains uncertain. The trajectory of education is shaped by myriad factors, and Unschooling's ultimate dominance is merely a speculative possibility. Yet, by engaging in these thought exercises, we invite dialogue and contemplation about the potential transformations that lie ahead.

Whether the future brings forth a Deschooled society or a different evolution altogether, it is our collective responsibility to continually reimagine and reevaluate our approach to education. Only by embracing innovation, fostering intellectual freedom, and nurturing a deep respect for individual learning journeys can we forge a path that empowers future generations to thrive and embrace the boundless possibilities that await them.

Empowering Education for All

Is Unschooling reserved for the privileged few? Not at all. Contrary to popular belief, Unschooling is not a luxury exclusive to the well-off and affluent. In fact, it can often be a more cost-effective alternative to traditional schooling.

When you choose to Unschool your child, you'll discover that the financial burden is significantly lighter compared to the expenses associated with sending them to a conventional school. There are no hefty tuition fees, costly uniforms, or extraneous expenses. Unschooling allows you to provide an education for your child within the comfort of your own home, with minimal financial strain.

Furthermore, communities around the world are teeming with free resources that can enrich your child's learning journey. Public libraries, for instance, offer a treasure trove of books, reference materials, and educational programs—all accessible at no cost. The abundance of knowledge and learning opportunities available within your community is truly remarkable.

And let's not forget the transformative power of the Internet. With a simple click of a button, a wealth of information is at your fingertips. Countless educational websites, online courses, and interactive platforms provide access to a vast array of subjects and resources. Unschoolers can tap into this digital realm, exploring new horizons and expanding their knowledge in ways that were unimaginable in the past.

Unschooling is not about material wealth or privilege—it is about embracing a different approach to education, one that values personalized learning, curiosity, and a deep connection with the world around us. It is within the reach of every family, regardless of their socioeconomic background.

Let go of the notion that Unschooling is only for the privileged few. Embrace the boundless possibilities that this educational path offers and embark on a journey of discovery and growth alongside your child. Unschooling is a transformative experience that transcends socioeconomic barriers, empowering families from all walks of life to provide an exceptional education rooted in passion, curiosity, and love.

Transforming Society

Unschooling is a radical movement that challenges the authority of the State and disrupts the traditional norms of education. It empowers individuals to take control of their own learning, liberating minds and cultivating independent thinking.

Instead of rebelling against the State, Unschooling seeks to strengthen the power of the people. It recognizes that true power lies within individuals and aims to unleash their full potential, intelligence, and freedom. By embracing Unschooling, individuals become active participants in their education, thinking critically, questioning authority, and making informed decisions.

Unschooling fosters a sense of self-reliance, autonomy, and personal responsibility. It encourages individuals to become independent thinkers and engaged citizens, contributing to the collective strength and intelligence of society. Rather than relying on the State for guidance, Unschooling nurtures the inherent power within individuals, transforming them into empowered learners.

Through Unschooling, individuals break free from the constraints of traditional schooling and discover the limitless possibilities of self-directed learning. They become architects of their own education, embracing their unique interests, passions, and talents. Unschooling allows individuals to explore diverse subjects, cultivate curiosity, and deepen their understanding of the world.

In this paradigm, the relationship between individuals and the State is reimagined. Unschooling demonstrates that education is not solely the domain of institutions but a personal journey that respects individual autonomy. It challenges the notion that the State should dictate the parameters of learning and emphasizes the importance of individual agency.

Unschooling is a catalyst for personal and societal transformation. It opens doors to new possibilities, encouraging individuals to think independently, innovate, and contribute to the betterment of society. By empowering individuals and transforming their educational experiences, Unschooling paves the way for a more vibrant, inclusive, and intellectually rich society.

In the realm of Unschooling, the power of the people shines brightly, as individuals embrace their potential and take ownership of their learning journey. It is a movement that embraces the inherent power within each person, forging a path towards personal liberation and a reimagined relationship between individuals and the State.

Embracing Diversity

Within the vibrant tapestry of the Unschooling community, there exists a diverse range of motivations and beliefs that guide parents on their educational journey. While most Unschoolers prioritize a well-rounded and secular education for their children, it is important to acknowledge that some hold strong religious convictions that influence their approach to teaching.

For a small subset of Unschoolers, their motivation stems from a desire to shield their children from certain secular curricula, such as the teaching of evolution. These parents firmly adhere to their religious beliefs and see it as their constitutional right to shape their child's education in alignment with their convictions. Legal precedents, such as the landmark case

"Wisconsin vs. Yoder" in 1972, have affirmed the rights of parents to uphold their religious values within the realm of education.

However, it is essential to recognize that the majority of Unschoolers embrace a secular approach to education, seeking to provide their children with a well-balanced and comprehensive understanding of the world. They understand the importance of equipping their children with the knowledge and critical thinking skills necessary to navigate an ever-evolving society.

Unschooling, at its core, promotes a deep appreciation for knowledge and the pursuit of truth. It encourages children to explore various subjects, engage with diverse perspectives, and develop their own understanding of the world. While parents may guide their children's educational journey, Unschooling is ultimately about fostering a love for learning and nurturing independent thinkers.

It is important to emphasize that Unschooling is not about isolating children from differing ideas or shielding them from critical scientific concepts. Instead, it encourages an open-minded approach, where children are exposed to a multitude of viewpoints, including those that may challenge their beliefs. By embracing this diversity of thought, Unschoolers empower their children to think critically, question assumptions, and engage in meaningful dialogue.

Unschooling is a celebration of intellectual curiosity and the pursuit of knowledge, regardless of one's religious or secular beliefs. It is a testament to the richness and depth of human understanding, where children are encouraged to explore the world with open hearts and inquisitive minds.

In the vast tapestry of Unschooling, each thread contributes to the vibrant mosaic of educational experiences. While motivations and beliefs may vary, the common thread that unites Unschoolers is a shared commitment to providing their children with a nurturing and intellectually stimulating environment, where they can flourish and become lifelong learners.

Chapter 11 – Unschooling Anywhere

Unschooling Across Borders

The allure of Unschooling knows no boundaries. While we often hear about its practice in the United States, the realm of self-directed education extends far beyond those borders, reaching the shores of other countries with its captivating philosophy.

Journeying northward to Canada, Unschooling, along with other forms of homeschooling, has found its rightful place. Across this vast nation, Unschooling thrives, offering families the freedom to craft their educational path in alignment with their values and aspirations. Each province has its own set of registration requirements, shaping the landscape of Unschooling with unique nuances.

In the pursuit of knowledge, we encounter the global tapestry of Unschooling. Its threads weave through diverse countries and cultures, where parents and children alike embrace the beauty of self-directed learning. From the enchanting landscapes of Europe to the vibrant communities of Australia and beyond, Unschooling manifests itself in unique ways, reflecting the spirit and values of each locale.

Broadening our horizons, we celebrate the universal appeal of Unschooling. Traversing borders, we immerse ourselves in the tapestry of educational diversity, recognizing that the quest for knowledge and the pursuit of lifelong learning transcend geographical boundaries. Whether in the United States, Canada, or any corner of the world, the essence of Unschooling remains a beacon of inspiration for those who dare to embrace an educational journey outside the traditional confines.

Embark on this global adventure, united by a shared commitment to nurturing the innate curiosity and love of learning that resides within every child, regardless of their geographical location.

Unschooling Down Under

In the vast expanse of Australia, the spirit of homeschooling has thrived through a remarkable institution known as the 'School of the Air'. This innovative approach to education, delivered via radio, has bridged the educational divide for children residing in remote cattle or sheep properties. Embracing the principles of parental involvement and the recognition of local learning opportunities, the School of the Air has left an indelible mark on the Australian educational landscape.

The echoes of this renowned institution have reverberated across the nation, fostering a deep appreciation for alternative educational paths. While the School of the Air catered to rural areas, its legacy has paved the way for the growing acceptance of Unschooling in

Australian families. Proudly embraced by communities and silently embraced by many, Unschooling has quietly emerged as a beacon of hope for those disillusioned with the traditional school system.

Australia's educational landscape mirrors the challenges faced by its American counterparts, leading an increasing number of families to explore the transformative realm of Unschooling. Though the journey may unfold discreetly, stories of individual experiences come to light, shedding a spotlight on the power of personalized education. One such tale is that of Rachael Clark, a Brisbane mother who turned to Unschooling when the traditional education system fell short for her children, as revealed in a thought-provoking article published on news.com.au.

As we delve into the unique educational fabric of Australia, we discover a nation brimming with possibilities. The land down under has embraced Unschooling as a quiet revolution, igniting the flames of change for those seeking an educational journey aligned with their values and aspirations. While the headlines may not scream of its presence, the spirit of Unschooling weaves its way through the hearts and minds of Australian families, transforming the educational landscape one child at a time.

Unschooling in New Zealand

In New Zealand, an educational revolution is quietly taking hold. A recent controversy has ignited a spirited dialogue, drawing attention to the burgeoning interest in alternative forms of education. At the heart of this movement lies a vibrant community of individuals embracing the principles of Unschooling.

Amidst breathtaking landscapes and a rich cultural tapestry, families in New Zealand are reimagining the way education is approached. They are questioning the traditional schooling system and seeking an alternative path that nurtures creativity, critical thinking, and individuality. Unschooling has become a beacon of hope for those who yearn for a more holistic and authentic learning experience.

In this remarkable journey, New Zealanders are embracing the idea that education extends far beyond the confines of a classroom. They understand that true learning can be found in the wonders of nature, the guidance of mentors, and the diverse tapestry of everyday life. Unschooling in New Zealand is not just an educational choice, but a lifestyle that encourages exploration, curiosity, and self-discovery.

As stories of these courageous pioneers spread across the land, a collective desire for change is ignited. Families are uniting in their pursuit of a more meaningful and relevant education for their children. They are determined to break free from the constraints of conventional schooling and embrace a path that allows their children's passions and talents to flourish.

New Zealand stands as a testament to the power of educational innovation. It is a place where the traditional boundaries of learning are challenged, and new possibilities are embraced. Unschooling is not just a passing trend; it is a paradigm shift that holds the potential to transform the educational landscape for generations to come.

In New Zealand, the future of learning is being shaped, one courageous step at a time.

Unschooling in the Boonies

Is unschooling more suited to people who live in rural areas? This question often arises, assuming that the countryside holds an advantage over urban areas when it comes to educational opportunities. However, I am here to debunk that notion and shed light on the richness of learning experiences that urban environments offer.

Urban areas, just like rural areas, are brimming with learning opportunities. The cityscape becomes a vibrant tapestry of knowledge, offering countless avenues to observe, study, engage, research, and fully immerse oneself in the learning journey. The diversity of urban life presents a plethora of experiences waiting to be explored.

While the specific learnings may differ, there is no hierarchy or prescribed set of knowledge that defines the Unschooling philosophy. Each individual's educational path is unique, and this inclusivity is what makes Unschooling so empowering. Why should your learning be forced to mirror mine? Embracing the diversity of learning experiences is at the heart of Unschooling.

So, whether you find yourself in a rural retreat or amidst the bustling city streets, know that both environments offer a wealth of educational opportunities. The key lies in cultivating a curious mindset, seizing the moments of discovery, and recognizing that learning can thrive anywhere.

Unschooling is not limited by geographic boundaries but is guided by the boundless spirit of exploration and growth. It is a testament to the fact that learning knows no constraints, and the world is our classroom, regardless of where we call home.

Taking the Unschooling Path

Embarking on the journey of unschooling with your child is an exciting and transformative experience. But how should you prepare for this unique educational approach? The answer is simple: start now.

Your child is already brimming with interests and passions, and they possess a natural curiosity and innate ability to learn. Embrace their existing knowledge and be guided by their desires. Unschooling thrives on the principle of following your child's lead, allowing their curiosity to shape their educational path.

As you begin this enlightening journey, I encourage you to be courageous. Release any fears or doubts that may hold you back.

Unschooling is not a path to be feared, but rather a liberating approach that nurtures your child's love for learning.

To deepen your understanding of unschooling, immerse yourself in literature that delves into its philosophy. Books, articles, and magazines like the Home Education Magazine (H.E.M.) published by www.unschooling.com can provide invaluable insights and guidance.

Furthermore, seek connection and support from other unschooling parents. Engage in online discussion groups, explore the comments sections of unschooling blogs, and embrace the opportunity to share experiences and wisdom. The collective knowledge and camaraderie of like-minded parents can be a powerful resource on this journey.

Remember, there is no one-size-fits-all approach to unschooling. Embrace the uniqueness of your child's educational journey, and trust in their innate ability to learn and grow. As you embark on this path, let curiosity be your compass and love be your guide.

Chapter 12 – Resources

Finding Support on the Journey

In the vast expanse of the Unschooling world, a warm embrace awaits parents seeking connection, guidance, and camaraderie. Within this vibrant community, numerous support groups, both national and local, flourish across the United States, offering a lifeline to Unschooling parents navigating this unconventional educational path.

These support groups serve as beacons of support, bringing together like-minded individuals who share a common vision for their children's education. They foster an environment of solidarity, where parents can exchange experiences, seek advice, and find encouragement along their Unschooling journey. For within this community, Unschooling is not a solitary endeavor; it is a collective effort driven by a shared commitment to empowering our children with the freedom to learn and grow authentically.

Within these support groups, an abundance of resources awaits, offering a wealth of knowledge and inspiration. From insightful articles and thought-provoking discussions to practical tips and personal anecdotes, these resources serve as guiding lights illuminating the path of Unschooling.

To embark on this journey of discovery, allow me to offer a curated selection of invaluable resources, crafted with the expertise and passion of Jennifer Grail from The Path Less Taken. These digital sanctuaries provide a sanctuary for Unschooling families, nurturing a sense of community, and delivering a wealth of wisdom and insights to aid parents on their Unschooling odyssey.

Joyfully Rejoicing
www.joyfullyrejoycing.com/
A heartfelt sanctuary of inspiration and guidance, filled with articles, stories, and resources to support and empower Unschooling families.

Sandra Dodd
sandradodd.com/unschooling
A treasure trove of Unschooling philosophy and practical advice, offering a wealth of resources for parents and children alike.

Learn in Freedom
learninfreedom.org
An empowering resource that explores the principles and benefits of Unschooling, equipping parents with knowledge and insights to navigate this educational path.

John Holt's Growing Without Schooling
johnholtgws.com/
A tribute to the pioneering work of John Holt, this platform offers a wealth of articles, archives, and resources that delve into the essence of Unschooling.

Within these digital realms, a chorus of voices resonates, guiding and uplifting Unschooling parents with wisdom and camaraderie. These resources, coupled with the unwavering support of fellow Unschoolers, provide a tapestry of inspiration and encouragement, nurturing the flame of educational freedom.

Take solace in the knowledge that you are not alone on this path. Embrace the support of these vibrant communities, delve into the treasure troves of knowledge they offer, and ask yourself: What knowledge and insights do I seek? What challenges do I wish to overcome? With these questions in mind, embark on a journey of exploration, for within these digital realms lie the keys to unlocking a world of Unschooling wisdom.

Immerse yourself in the heartfelt articles, personal stories, and thought-provoking discussions found in these virtual havens. Absorb the experiences and perspectives shared by fellow Unschooling parents who have traversed similar paths. Draw inspiration from their triumphs, find solace in their challenges, and discover innovative approaches to tailor your Unschooling journey to the unique needs and interests of your children.

As you delve deeper into these resources, you will encounter a wealth of practical advice, innovative ideas, and creative learning strategies. Unschooling is not a rigid set of rules, but a fluid and dynamic approach that embraces the natural curiosity and innate love of learning within each child. Let these resources guide you in creating an environment where your children can explore their passions, cultivate critical thinking skills, and forge their own educational paths.

In addition to the valuable insights gleaned from these digital spaces, the support groups themselves are a wellspring of connection and camaraderie. Reach out to fellow Unschooling parents, engage in discussions, and build relationships that transcend virtual boundaries. Share your triumphs and challenges, seek guidance, and offer support to others on their Unschooling journeys. Together, we can foster a community of growth, empowerment, and mutual respect.

Remember that Unschooling is not just an educational choice; it is a transformative lifestyle that celebrates the inherent curiosity and potential within every child. By embracing the resources and support available to you, you embark on a remarkable adventure of self-discovery, intellectual growth, and joyous learning.

So, let the vibrant Unschooling community be your guiding light, illuminating the path towards educational liberation and embracing the power of self-directed learning. Embrace wisdom, forge connections, and journey onward, knowing that you are part of a movement that empowers parents and children to create a future filled with endless possibilities. Together, we can reshape the landscape of education and inspire generations to come.

The Treasures of Unschooling

If you're eager to dive deeper into the captivating realm of unschooling, there are a plethora of resources waiting to ignite your curiosity and expand your understanding. Let me be your guide as we embark on this enlightening journey.

First and foremost, immerse yourself in the wisdom of renowned authors who have paved the way for unschooling. Ivan Illich, Everett Reimer, John Gatto, and John Holt have gifted us with profound insights into alternative education. Their influential works are readily available online, allowing you to delve into their captivating writings and unlock the secrets of unschooling. So grab a cup of tea, find a cozy spot, and let their words transport you into a world of radical educational possibilities.

But the adventure doesn't stop there. Head over to YouTube, a treasure trove of interviews and documentaries that delve into the depths of unschooling. Explore the vibrant discussions featuring the inspiring voices of Gatto and Holt as they shed light on the transformative power of self-directed learning. Prepare to be captivated as you witness firsthand accounts and thought-provoking narratives that will challenge your perceptions of traditional education.

For those seeking tangible resources, your local library is a gateway to a wealth of knowledge. Don't miss the opportunity to dive into John Holt's seminal works, *"How Children Fail"* and *"How Children Learn."* These timeless classics offer profound insights into the learning process and the importance of nurturing a child's innate curiosity and love for learning.

And as the unschooling movement continues to flourish, a myriad of new books are published each year, catering to the needs and aspirations of those interested in embarking on the unschooling path. Seek out these invaluable resources, as they serve as guiding lights on your transformative journey.

I also invite you to explore my own contribution to this extraordinary world of education. "The Smartest Kids Learn All the Time" and "The Smartest Kids Know School Stinks" are my heartfelt explorations of the transformative power of unschooling, delving into the experiences and insights that have shaped our lives. Allow my words to inspire and empower you as you embrace the unschooling philosophy.

Are you ready to unravel the mysteries of unschooling? To embrace the words of the visionaries who have walked this path before us. I invite you to immerse yourself in captivating books, websites, and documentaries, and discover the boundless potential that unschooling holds.

May you unlock the true essence of education, igniting a flame that illuminates a future where the pursuit of knowledge transcends all boundaries.

"Our form of schooling has turned us into dependent, emotionally needy, excessively childish people who wait for a teacher to tell them what to do. Our national dilemma is that too many of us are now homeless and mindless in the deepest sense - at the mercy of strangers. The beginning of answers will come only when people force government to return educational choice to everyone."

As we bid farewell, let us reflect on the profound words of John Gatto. With clarity and conviction, he exposes the flaws of our current schooling system, highlighting the detrimental effects it has on our independence and intellectual growth. His poignant observation reminds us of the pressing national crisis we face, where too many individuals find themselves adrift, lacking purpose and at the mercy of external forces. The path to change begins with reclaiming our educational autonomy, demanding that the government restore the power of choice to all. May these words resonate in your journey, inspiring you to challenge the status quo and shape a future where true education knows no bounds. Good luck on your transformative quest!

About the Author

Kytka Hilmar-Jezek stands as a highly accomplished author, renowned for her influential books that have left an indelible mark on readers. With a focus on parenting, education, entrepreneurship, and natural healing, her extensive repertoire of over twenty-five thought-provoking works has earned her widespread recognition, including a place in the Revolution in Education Hall of Fame.

Kytka's passion for education shines through her books, which boldly challenge conventional schooling paradigms and stimulate discussions on alternative approaches. Notable titles such as "The Smartest Kids Don't Go to School," "The Smartest Kids Learn All the Time," and "The Smartest Kids Know School Stinks" offer fresh perspectives, urging readers to question traditional norms and embrace innovative methods of nurturing children in the technological age.

Her debut book, "Reiki for Children," quickly soared to become a global bestseller in 2001, resonating with professionals in the field who employ it as a valuable resource in teaching children. Expanding her healing-focused publications, Hilmar-Jezek has authored works like "Raw Food for Children," "Eat the Light: The Raw Food Diet as a Spiritual Practice," "The Ultimate Beginner's Guide to Reiki," and "The Rainbow Tower," a captivating exploration of Chakras designed for young readers.

Kytka's engaging books consistently enlighten, inspire, and challenge readers on controversial and thought-provoking subjects related to health and wellness, parenting, spirituality, and education. Through her publishing houses, Distinct Press and Czech Revival Publishing, she actively promotes diverse voices across various literary genres, fostering a platform for aspiring authors to share their unique perspectives. With her remarkable versatility, she has ghostwritten over 200 books for clients worldwide and translated more than 100 books from the Czech language.

Kytka Hilmar-Jezek's journey as an accomplished author and book editor is marked by an unwavering dedication to exploring unconventional approaches to education, parenting, health, and personal growth. Her thought-provoking books, advocacy for diverse voices, and commitment to preserving cultural heritage have made a profound impact on the literary world. By delving into her works, readers embark on a transformative journey that challenges norms, inspires critical thinking, and fosters positive change in their lives and communities.

Outside her literary endeavors, Kytka finds joy in various ventures, such as her contributions to TresBohemes.com, where she has penned numerous posts on Czech culture. Her commitment to preserving cultural heritage is further evident in her work preserving old photographs for The Photo Vault and curating items for The Czech Museum. Most of all, she loves to read on lazy afternoons, snuggled next to her Shiba Inu, Richard.

Learn more at kytkajezek.com.

www.ingramcontent.com/pod-product-compliance
Lightning Source LLC
Chambersburg PA
CBHW032030090426
42733CB00029B/71